J. a. R. Finlay.

The Countryman Nature Book

Waders at high tide — Hilbre Island, Cheshire
Knots and one redshank, oyster-catchers and
one bar-tailed godwit

The Countryman Nature Book

AN ANTHOLOGY FROM THE COUNTRYMAN

Edited by RICHARD FITTER

Director: Intelligence Unit of the Council for Nature

Brockhampton Press LEICESTER

First published in 1960
by Brockhampton Press Ltd
Market Place, Leicester
Made and printed in Great Britain
by Jarrold & Sons Ltd, Norwich
Copyright © 1960 by The Countryman Ltd

Contents

The Countryman is a quarterly magazine whose editorial address is Burford, Oxford. Copies may be obtained from 10 Bouverie Street, London E.C.4

Foreword

In the old days nobody believed any fact that they had not read in the works of Aristotle or some other ancient writer. One Italian astronomer even went so far as to refuse to look through Galileo's telescope at his newly discovered moons because, he said, he knew they were not there. The idea of direct observation, of looking to see for oneself what the stars were doing or how animals behaved, was the great modern discovery, the keystone of scientific development in the past 400 years.

We still know hardly anything about the life history and behaviour of the great majority of animals and plants, even in the British Isles. This is not surprising, for to take three groups of insects alone, there are some 6,300 kinds of bees, wasps and ichneumons and their allies, 5,200 different two-winged flies and 3,700 beetles in some part or other of these small islands. This means that there is always immense scope for any individual to add to the stock of human knowledge by personal observations, even in his or her own garden. And, of course, to get a great deal of enjoyment in the process.

All the notes, articles and photographs in this book were originally published in *The Countryman*, and they are all based on personal observation, mostly by people who would never think of calling themselves naturalists. I very much hope that some readers of these fascinating true stories will themselves be tempted to go out and watch wild creatures, whether birds, beasts or insects and will perhaps note down some of the things they see.

RICHARD FITTER

Butterflies in Britain Today

by L. Hugh Newman

THERE can be no doubt that during the last ten or fifteen years butterflies have declined greatly in numbers. The reasons for the decline are many and complex. Enormous areas of what was once countryside have been built over, and the meadows where butterflies could breed have disappeared under tarmac and houses. Occasionally collectors are blamed, but in the opinion of scientific entomologists over-collecting has rarely been a direct cause of the decline. I can think of only one glaring example: the extinction of the large copper from the Fens. Man is undoubtedly to blame, but not individual men. Our way of life, industrial expansion, building activities and new methods of agriculture and forestry all combine to make Britain a less congenial place for butterflies than it used to be. Many of the places which I remember as being pleasantly scrubby and filled with wild flowers before the war are now regularly cultivated.

Efficient farming is praiseworthy; there can be no doubt about that. But one aspect of progress has dismayed many naturalists: the extensive use of toxic sprays as weedkillers and insecticides. The latter especially kill both the good and the bad; bees, butterflies and many other harmless or directly useful insects perish with the pests. The spraying of roadside verges with weedkillers is perhaps the greatest crime which has been committed, mainly by county councils as highway authorities. Labour-saving has always been the excuse, but the results have been so deplorable that public opinion has been aroused. In my own road, in a residential area, the council employed a firm to spray the weeds along the edges of the tarmac pavements, and within six months a long row of double flowering cherries began to die. Then a gang of men came along to uproot the trees which had given so much pleasure every spring. Happily this indiscriminate spraying, which two years ago had even extended to narrow country lanes, has now been abandoned, and only trunk and Class 1 roads are being treated. Untold damage was done, and is still being done, to insect life by the practice. The road verges, when left to themselves or cut once in the season, are a mass of grasses and wild flowers, pleasant to look on and ideal breeding grounds for quite a number of butterflies; and as the amount of waste land elsewhere decreases, the importance of these narrow strips grows.

Deciduous woodlands are the home of several species of butterfly, especially the fritillaries, and whenever a stretch of forest is felled they lose a breeding ground which cannot be replaced. Conifers are usually planted so close together that the ground vegetation disappears and the forest become useless for butterflies. Only where the Forestry Commission has planted hardwoods can we hope to see the silver-washed and high brown fritillaries again, and then only if there is a chance of their spreading from some neighbouring woodland. They are not butterflies which travel for any distance, and if their haunts are destroyed they will die out. Quite recently, near Eynsford in Kent, I visited a wood which was an ideal spot for pearl-bordered and small pearl-bordered fritillaries. It used to be coppiced quite regularly, and plenty of violets grew in the dappled shade. The trees had been uprooted and burnt, and the ground churned up as if huge prehistoric beasts had been fighting over it; shortly the whole area would be ploughed and incorporated in the farmland surrounding it. Any hibernating insects would most certainly have perished, and there must be many similar instances in other counties.

Quite apart from human activities the butterfly population is undoubtedly affected by factors over which we have no control, and the most important is the weather. More than most other insects butterflies need sun and warmth. If the weather is unfavourable for long periods they will not fly, feed or mate, and a heavy reduction in numbers will quickly become apparent. If two consecutive generations, such as the early and late broods of some species of blue, have the misfortune to emerge during cold rainy spells the whole race can be practically exterminated in that area. One bad summer following another can mean that butterflies will be scarce for a decade or more.

A pair of
small pearl-
bordered
fritillaries
courting

The gadfly's tool for the job

A green hairstreak butterfly on a bird's-eye primrose

Three freak and one normal blue from Royston Heath

A white-letter hairstreak

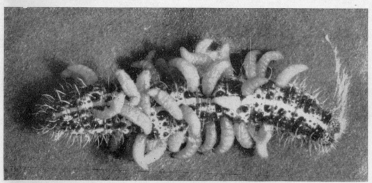

Ichneumon-fly grubs emerging from a living caterpillar. Three minutes later all the grubs had turned into pupæ in cocoons of bright yellow silk (see page 15)

A cold winter will generally do far less damage than a sunless rainy summer, but when the cold lasts for an unusually long time, as in the winter of 1946–7, it can be disastrous. A friend of mine who has a large shoot in Sussex is convinced that the fritillaries there were almost wiped out that spring. Not only were the hibernating larvæ unable to start feeding at the usual time, but when the snow did finally melt it thawed so rapidly that violets on sloping ground were washed away in a sea of mud in which no caterpillar could survive. Conversely, too mild a winter can be harmful, especially to butterflies which hibernate. I am sure that the warm winter of 1956–7 was partly to blame for the following summer's dearth of small tortoiseshells and peacocks. Many awoke from hibernation too soon, came out into the warm sunlight and died when the weather turned cold again, having failed to find any nourishment. When the time came for egg-laying their numbers were already depleted, and the exceptionally heavy aphis infestation in the spring and early summer must have prevented innumerable broods of caterpillars from gaining maturity. In my own district most of the nettle beds were so heavily attacked that the leaves of the plants were completely coated by dense masses of the repulsive little insects. Even if the butterflies' eggs were not sucked dry, the newly hatched caterpillars were unable to feed. The second generation of small tortoiseshells had a better chance, but even so the species will probably take several years to build up its numbers again.

Late spring frosts can affect the populations of some kinds of butterfly, especially those which feed on the young foliage of susceptible shrubs and trees. The purple and white-letter hairstreaks both spend the winter in the egg stage, and the larvæ hatch as soon as the buds unfold on oaks and wych elms, on which they feed. If the leaves get 'burnt' the larvæ die. This was particularly noticeable in the spring of 1956 when, motoring to the coast through Sussex, I saw woods and coppices where the purple hairstreak breeds blackened by frost. In at least one locality in Surrey the late frost almost exterminated the white-letter hairstreak.

Ichneumon flies play a large part in the fluctuations of the butterfly population. It has been known for a long time that the numbers of butterflies in an area rise and fall in more or less regular cycles, the peak being reached about once in twenty years. This variation in numbers is linked with fluctuations in the number of parasites and in the ordinary way would not lead to the complete disappearance of a species. The danger comes when other adverse influences, such as bad weather or man's interference, happen to coincide with a trough period; if the population then falls below survival level it is unable to build up again and the colony dies out.

Virus diseases are common among butterflies and moths, and latent virus is nearly always present. Adverse conditions will activate it and, though it is difficult to determine exactly what these conditions are, it seems that humidity plays an important part. Outbreaks of virus are not at all uncommon in the wild, and I have often found broods of small tortoiseshell and peacock caterpillars in a dying condition. When an outbreak like this occurs – and it did occur, at least in my district, in the summers of 1957 and 1958 – the number of butterflies will obviously decline noticeably.

Another more mysterious occurrence which apparently indicates a serious weakening of the race, possibly by some form of hereditary disease, is the sudden appearance of a great number of abnormally marked specimens in a colony. The most famous instance of this occurred at Royston Heath at the end of the 1914–18 war, when the chalkhill blues which swarmed there produced an unprecedented number of fine varieties. Collectors came from all over the country to capture these freaks, which continued to appear in increasing numbers for four or five years. Then the colony suddenly died out almost completely. Ichneumon flies seem to have been partly responsible, but such a total collapse of an unusually numerous colony in a single year must have been the result of a combination of adverse factors. The Dover race of blues, which many years ago produced a high percentage of specimens with 'shot-holed' wings and then died out mysteriously, must have been another local race in decline through some congenital heredity defect.

Of all our insects butterflies are undoubtedly the most beautiful, and it is a sad thought that our children may not see 'fields of butterflies' as we did in our youth; but the picture is not an entirely gloomy one. At least two species have not only maintained their numbers but increased them quite remarkably in my lifetime. The comma, which in my boyhood was scarce and confined mainly to the West Country, can now be found all over southern England; and the white admiral, no longer a woodland rarity, appears even on the outskirts of London.

SUDDEN EXODUS

by H. H. Goodchild

On several occasions I have found the shrunken and perforated skin of a large white butterfly's caterpillar from which ichneumon-fly grubs have emerged. The female fly deposits twenty to forty eggs in the caterpillar. These hatch into minute grubs, which start immediately to burrow into the substance of their host and eventually attain a length of about 6 mm.

Infected caterpillars seem quite healthy and feed voraciously, so they must do at least as much damage as others, although they never reach the chrysalis stage. Wishing to see and photograph the emergence of the grubs I selected six caterpillars, all of which had stopped feeding and appeared ready to pupate; and I arranged each on a piece of card, ready to place under my camera.

After several hours I noticed that one had developed a number of minute white spots along the whole length of its body; these gave the first indication that the grubs were about to emerge. Within thirty seconds some two dozen had made

their way out, and at the end of three minutes all had turned into pupæ clothed in cocoons of bright yellow silk. The photograph on page 12 shows the grubs leaving their host. A possible explanation of the simultaneous exodus occurred to me later. Opening a caterpillar just before the parasites were ready to escape, I found that attached to the posterior of each was a small bladder filled with a clear liquid; but no grub that had escaped naturally bore any trace of the bladder, which presumably had emptied as it escaped. This suggested that the bladders contained a liquid obnoxious to the grubs, which were driven out as soon as the first was ruptured.

The liquid may also have anæsthetized the caterpillar, for it gave no sign of life while the grubs were boring their way out. Only four or five hours later did it move, climbing on top of the nearest group of cocoons; it had then recovered sufficiently to swing its head from side to side when touched. I kept a number of caterpillars under observation after the parasites had escaped, and all died, after regaining consciousness, within three to five days.

A Lace-Wing's Egg Hatches

by C. B. Williams

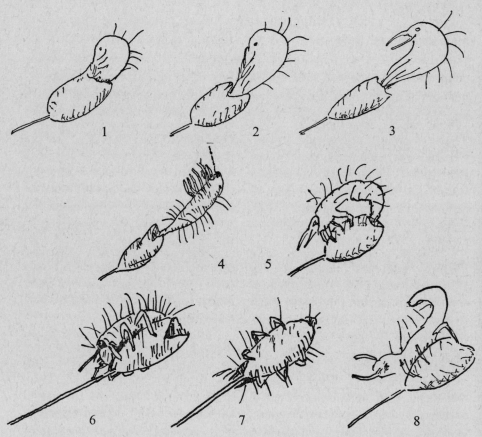

ON the undersides of leaves one may find tiny white eggs, smaller than the smallest pin-head, each on the end of a hair-like stalk up to an inch in length. There are often a dozen or more on one leaf, forming a miniature forest. These are the eggs of the green lace-wing flies, a group of Neuroptera known scientifically as Chrysopidæ, and also popularly called green stink-flies, because of the strong scent which they emit. They are predaceous in both young and adult stages, feeding on green-fly and other small insects and their eggs, so that they are beneficial to the gardener. I had often seen these eggs and wondered what exactly happened when they hatched out, and the young grubs found themselves in a strange world sitting on the end of a tall flagpole. Did they crawl along the stalk or jump?

One day I was examining some eggs under a low-power binocular microscope, and found that they were just in the process of hatching. I was able to observe the whole process from start to finish under ideal conditions, and made a series of rapid sketches which are reproduced here in the order of occurrence. I noticed the egg hatching at about 12.30 and the first sketch was made a few minutes later. It shows the young larva, having just broken the eggshell, pushing out backwards, but the antennæ, jaws and legs are not yet free. The second sketch shows the jaws free of the shell, but not yet separated. In the third the jaws are free of the body, and the legs practically free of the shell. The sucker tail has a grip within the shell. This is emphasized still more by the next stage (4) in which the larva lay out almost horizontally from the eggshell on its back, held only by the tail still within the shell. Five or ten minutes were spent in this position presumably for some hardening process and then the larva swung round on top of the egg and clung on with its legs, its tail being still within the egg (5, 6 and 7). At this stage there was again a rest, and it was not until thirty-five minutes after I first saw the egg hatching that the tail was withdrawn from it and waved about in the air (8).

The larva then settled down for a long rest, and an hour later it was still in the same position. Shortly after, however, it became active, and crawled down the stalk of the egg to the leaf. Although its movements were slow and deliberate, it never stopped crawling until it reached the bottom, and my powers of rapid drawing were not equal to making an adequate sketch of it during this activity. But I had seen a lace-wing's egg hatch, and found the answer to my question, as to how the larva got away from the egg.

Ladybird Swarms

by C. B. Williams

EARLY in November, some years ago, one of the farm staff at Rothamsted Experimental Station reported that large numbers of small ladybird beetles had settled on a gate-post. I had heard many times of such aggregations (usually, but not always, associated with hibernation), but had never seen one, so I set off immediately with a colleague for the site. The gate opened north and south, and on the southern face of one of the stout wooden posts there were three or four thousand ladybirds; only a few hundred were on the other three faces, but there were several thousand more in the grass at the foot of the post and, for a short distance, of the wire fence, again mostly on the south side. On the other post of the same gate there were about thirty, and on a gate-post twenty yards away not a single one. The beetles were in bunches of from three or four up to several hundred, in a single layer, as the photograph shows. They were the sixteen-spot ladybird, but of a variety with only twelve spots. Both males and females were present, the former slightly predominating.

At first we thought that the swarm had formed prior to hiding away in some hole or well-protected spot for the winter, and we arranged to watch it every day to see when the final movement took place, and, if possible, to trace its destination. To our surprise, day after day passed without any diminution in numbers or evidence of movement away from the post, until the end of the year. In late December and January there were falls of snow, and each resulted in a considerable reduction in the numbers; but, even after the second, about four hundred remained, exposed to the weather, on the south side of the post. Through one part of it there was an old bolt-hole, but none entered this for protection. The number varied from four hundred to seven hundred during January,

February and March, but dropped rapidly about the middle of April; by the beginning of May nearly all had gone. Throughout the winter the beetles climbed up the post in warm weather, and went lower and were more numerous on the grass in bad weather, but several hundreds braved the worst of the season without making any attempt to seek shelter.

There are other records of ladybirds congregated together, which do not seem to be connected with hibernation. Fabre records the finding of great numbers on stones at the top of the Puy de Dôme in France. I have had several cases reported to me in Egypt, including one in which a party of surveyors in the desert returned to their camp one evening to find the tent covered with thousands of ladybirds. The tent ropes were 'twice the normal diameter' owing to the layers of beetles settled on them, and a bath sponge inside the tent had every hole full of them. The locality was marked on the map unofficially as Ladybird Valley.

The Language of Bees

by Colin G. Butler

ALMOST all the information we possess about the methods by which bees communicate with each other has come to us through the genius of Professor Karl von Frisch. He was the first to demonstrate conclusively that there is a 'language' of bees, and has also carried out virtually all of the later experimental work which has elucidated a part of it. Owing to the great advances which he has made in this line of research during the last few years, we are beginning to feel that, although we do not possess by any means a complete understanding of bee language, we know something of its basic form.

As long ago as 1923, von Frisch showed that worker honey-bees are able to inform one another about a source of food by means of a dance, of which there are two extreme patterns. In the 'round' dance, the bee runs round in a circle on the comb, first in one direction and then in the other, thus tracing out a figure of eight in which the two loops are more or less closely superimposed on each other. The figure-of-eight pattern is also followed in the 'wagtail' dance, but with the two loops of the eight separated by a straight run, during the making of which the dancer wags her abdomen rapidly from side to side. It was supposed at first that these were two quite distinct dances; that by the round dance a foraging bee which had found a good source of nectar was able to inform her sisters of its presence somewhere outside the hive; and that similarly, by the wagtail dance, she was able to tell them about a source of pollen. Later it was found that the information given by the dancer is a little more precise than this; the perfume of the flower from which the nectar or pollen has been collected is noticed, either on the dancer's body or in the sips of nectar which she gives from time to time, by the other bees, which become interested in her antics. Thus, by 1923 it had been shown

A bee prepares to land on a salvia flower.

Deep in the flower the bee sets in action the tongue-
shaped anthers loaded with pollen. *Above*, the pollen
is pressed against the bee's back

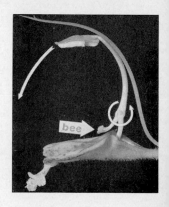

that, when a bee finds a good source of food outside her hive, she often dances on her return, the vigour of the dances depending on the source's richness; and that other bees of foraging age are attracted by the dancing and, having perceived the perfume, leave the hive in search of it. These bees seek flowers so perfumed in all directions round the hive and, by finding them in the end, discover the source of food.

Until 1946 when von Frisch published two epoch-making papers, it was not thought that the dancing bee could indicate the direction and distance of the source of food from the hive. It is now known, however, that she gives precise information on these points. The failure to discover this earlier was due largely to the fact that it was incorrectly believed that the round dance was concerned solely with the collection of nectar, and the wagtail one with that of pollen. Now we know that the wagtail dance is nothing more than an extension of the round one, and that either may indicate the presence of nectar or pollen. If the source is situated within about a hundred yards of the hive, a round dance is performed; if it lies at a greater distance, the dance is a wagtail one. The number of straight runs of the wagtail dance – or, what amounts to the same thing, the number of complete figures of eight performed in a given time – indicate the distance of the food from the hive. The greater the distance, the longer the straight run, and the smaller the number of figures of eight completed per minute. Direction is indicated, on the vertical comb, by the angle at which the straight run is made. If it is made straight upwards on the comb, the food lies in the same direction as the sun; if downwards, away from the sun; if at an angle to the left of the perpendicular, at the same angle to the left of the sun; and so on. Thus, the angle of the straight run to the perpendicular varies for the same feeding place at different times of the day.

Sometimes, instead of dancing on the vertical face of a comb, bees will dance on the more or less horizontal alighting board of the hive. In these circumstances the straight run of the wagtail dance is made in the actual direction in which the source of food lies. Recently von Frisch has described how he used to observe the bees on the left-hand side of the comb in his glass-walled observation hive, the entrance of which is at the end of the combs. He found that, if the hive entrance faces east, the bees tend to indicate a place that is south of the correct feeding point; if west, a place too far to the north. If the entrance is turned towards the south, so that the combs run north and south, the bees tend to indicate a place too far south in the morning; but as the day progresses this error decreases in size, until at midday it has disappeared; during the afternoon it becomes more and more pronounced again, but this time with a bias towards the north. Thus it seemed probable that the light illuminating the comb under observation was the cause of this error. Fortunately a deep red light is invisible to the honey-bee, so the theory that the white light shining on the comb causes the error can be confirmed by making observations by red light only. Under such conditions the direction is indicated perfectly throughout the day. If, on the other hand, the comb is illuminated with a beam of unfiltered light from a powerful electric torch, the orientation of the dance varies as the angle of the light reaching the comb changes. It is clear, therefore, that within the darkness of the hive the dancing bee orientates herself to gravity, whereas on the alighting board she does it to light of some kind.

If an observation hive is so arranged that it can be turned about its horizontal axis, some interesting observations can be made. Though the bee on the vertical comb, which is exposed to daylight, is influenced in her dancing by this light, she none the less orientates herself primarily to gravity. If we turn the hive so that the face of a comb on which a bee is dancing comes to be downward, the dancer becomes very agitated and completely loses her sense of direction and gives up dancing. If we turn the comb so that it comes to lie in a horizontal position face uppermost, the dancer immediately reorientates herself to light rather than gravity, and makes the straight run of her dance in the direction of the source of food. If the comb is now turned gradually back to its normal vertical position, the influence of the light on the dancer becomes progressively less and that of gravity increases.

Now it has also been observed that bees will continue to dance and to indicate direction accurately, even when the sun is obscured by clouds so that its position cannot be observed properly. If the light from the sky, which is reaching a bee dancing on a horizontal surface, is filtered in such a way as to cut off all the ultra-violet light, the bee still dances properly; similarly, if the red end of the spectrum (including the infra-red) is cut off from the dancer, she continues to indicate direction correctly. Therefore it is clear that she is not orientating herself to heat rays or to light which is not visible to man.

It has been found that, if a bee is to dance on a horizontal surface, she must be able to see clear sky. Her 'window' need be only a few centimetres square, but, if this small area is progressively obscured, she becomes confused and more and more uncertain in her direction indication, and finally stops dancing altogether. Von Frisch is naturally cautious because he does not yet consider that he has obtained sufficient evidence to settle the matter, but he makes the revolutionary suggestion that honey-bees can appreciate the degree and plane of polarization of the light reflected from a blue sky. Since the light thus reflected is partly polarized – that is to say, the light waves, instead of vibrating in all planes at once, vibrate mainly in a single plane – and since the degree and plane of polarization vary in different parts of the sky, the honey-bee possesses in the sky a map by which to plot her course. Bees stop dancing when the sky becomes covered with dense cloud.

The more one studies the means by which bees communicate and their methods of finding their way about, the more one is amazed at the efficiency with which Nature achieves her ends.

HUNGRY WASPS

Two years ago we had four wasps' nests in the garden; two were taken, but the other two, which were in the bottom of a wall and had wide entrances, were difficult to deal with. The wasps attacked any insect that came near, and bees and bluebottles feeding on the same bush of ivy suffered casualties every few minutes. Sometimes two wasps would attack a bluebottle, bear it to the ground, dismember it and carry off the body in a few seconds.

On one occasion a wasp set about a honey-bee and rolled it over and over, until it got the bee pinned down on its back for a moment. It then stung it rapidly between its segments, the bee struggling furiously all the time, trying in vain to get home with its own sting. But the wasp was too nimble and eventually managed to bite the bee's sting off at its base. After that the bee soon became still except for its legs, which twitched spasmodically for some time.

A. F. Burgess, York

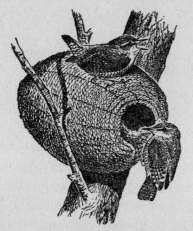

WREN AND BUMBLE-BEE by F. C. Archer

In a recent summer, as a variation of the ordinary nesting-box, I plaited long pieces of string and stitched them together in the form of a globular 'vase' with an opening about an inch across. This I fixed on its side in the fork of a lilac bush about 6 feet from the dining-room window. On March 23, a wren spent all day carefully examining the 'box' and testing its strength, particularly round the entrance, with its beak. Two days later this bird started to carry materials to it, and by the evening had built an inner wall, thus reducing the aperture by more than half. For the next three weeks it was in and out of the 'box' spasmodically and spent much time sitting on top of it, singing loudly and clearly. Occasionally it took inside minute portions of moss, and it roosted there each night. On April 12 two wrens appeared and spent the morning coquetting excitedly, singing lustily and dashing in and out of the nest. At midday they began to collect feathers and other light materials, and continued to do this on the two following days.

On April 15 only one bird appeared, going in and out, and occasionally spending about ten minutes in the nest. The following morning I saw a wren fly suddenly from under a bush nearby and go straight to the nest, but it did not go inside; it hung on to the entrance, poked its head in and out with jerky movements and began to flutter round the entrance, evidently in a state of great excitement. Suddenly it flew away, and out of the nest came a large bumble-bee which, for the rest of the day, appeared to return hourly. The wren came back at intervals, but only twice did it enter the nest, and then for no more than a few seconds. It continued to pay occasional visits, when it would cling on the entrance and appear to view the interior anxiously; sometimes it sat on top of the nest singing lustily, sometimes on a nearby branch. The bees, however, retained possession until August. No wren then went near the nest until October, when one visited it several times, hopping all round, sitting on it and carefully inspecting it. In the third week it began to clean out the 'box', and when the cold weather and snow came in mid-November it started to roost there regularly. A month later it was joined by another wren, and they roosted there together.

Bird-nesting for Insects

by G. E. Woodroffe and B. J. Southgate

WHEN nests are in hedges or trees, exposure to the weather results in alternate saturation and drying, so that they soon decay. These conditions are not suitable for many insects, but a nest that is protected to some extent from the weather provides an excellent source of food for the scavenging insects which also attack our food and clothing. Thus the nests of sparrows, starlings, martins and swifts on houses, of tits in holes, of swallows, robins and wrens on barns and outhouses, and of flycatchers and wagtails in old walls, form natural reservoirs of a number of household pests. It is the situation, not the kind of bird, that is important, except when two kinds differ in habits as regards cleanliness. Sparrows are notoriously dirty. Their nests become heavily soiled with droppings and a broken egg or two; they usually rear three broods during the summer and roost in the nests throughout the year. Consequently these are very nutritious to scavenging insects, of which they support a vast population. However, quite a number of insects are found in the comparatively clean blackbird's nest if, as sometimes happens, it has been built in a shed or in a creeper on a sheltered wall.

Let us imagine that a pair of sparrows has reared three broods under the eaves. We have borrowed a long ladder, removed the nest carefully and pulled it apart over a white enamel tray. When all the coarse straw has been well shaken and removed, we are left with a heap of dust and the smaller pieces of the nest material. If we then place the tray under an electric lamp, the warmth will drive out many of the insects.

The first to appear will need no description. They will hop in characteristic fashion and should be avoided because, although they are bird fleas, they will bite human beings when hungry. The very small, white maggots which may be found among the finer dust are immature fleas, and squirm and lash about frantically under the warmth of the lamp.

Next, probably, will come the spider-beetles. They may be of several kinds, but all are round-bodied, long-legged beetles with either golden or brown and white hairs on their backs. Their grubs are crescent-shaped, fat, white and hairy, and as they move very little they must be sought in the heap of dust and rubbish. One of the golden beetles, the Australian spider-beetle, is an important pest in warehouses and may also occur in domestic food stores.

Most of the other insects in the nest will be present in their immature stages: the moths, for example, as caterpillars, and the beetles as grubs. The most conspicuous caterpillar is that of the brown house-moth, and it is usually found in hundreds. It is a fat, white caterpillar, about an inch long, very glossy, and with a chestnut-brown head and a paler brown shield on the body segment immediately behind the head. Smaller than this, dull instead of glossy and with a darker brown shield, but otherwise similar, is the caterpillar of the white-shouldered house-moth. These have been described as the commonest moths to be found indoors in Britain. They are about half an inch long, and narrow when their wings are folded. The brown house-moth is brown, spotted with darker brown, while the white-shouldered one has wings mottled with various shades of grey, and a pure white head and shoulders. Both are well known pests of stored foods, especially of grain and seeds, and both, particularly the brown, may damage woollen materials and carpets.

The common clothes-moth is the very small, plain, shining gold one that is familiar to everyone. Its caterpillars may be found in only small numbers in our nest. They are smaller than those of the house-moths, move more quickly and have no brown shield behind the head. The other important species is the case-bearing clothes-moth, which is slightly larger, more grey than gold in colour, and has one or three indistinct darker grey patches on it wings. The name is derived from the fact that its caterpillars spin themselves small silk cocoons which they carry round with them. They enlarge them as they grow and leave them only when they emerge from the chrysalis as moths. When the heap of nest rubbish has been thoroughly warmed up, we shall see thousands of these little caterpillars humping their cocoons along with only their front half protruding from one end.

Next we come to the carpet-beetles. There are several kinds, but it is often difficult to distinguish between them, so we will confine ourselves to the two commonest. The grubs of the varied carpet-beetle are certain to walk out of our pile of dust. They are about a quarter of an inch long, brown in colour and furry, with little tufts of hairs (like the tufts of bristles in a tooth-brush) at the tail end; these are fanned out to form rosettes when the creature is alarmed. The beetles are like small brown ladybirds, with lighter flecks on the back. They can be found on the flowers of hogweed in early summer. The grubs, or 'woolly bears' as they are often called, attack clothing and are probably responsible for some of the damage blamed on clothes-moths. We may also find the grubs of the fur-beetle – handsome creatures, often three-quarters of an inch long and shaped like torpedoes, with tails of long hairs. They are gold in colour and, when full grown, are ringed with bronze. The beetle is dark brown and shiny, with two round white dots in the middle of the back. Like the varied carpet-beetle, the fur-beetle is a pest of clothing and upholstered furniture.

Finally, mention must be made of the yellow meal-worm, which is too familiar to need description, although the dark brown beetle into which the 'worm' develops is less well known. We should probably find several dozen full-grown meal-worms in our sparrow's nest, as well as many smaller ones. The meal-worm is a minor pest of cereals in Britain.

The insects to be found in birds' nests can be divided into two main groups: those associated with the birds, and those whose business is with the nest. To the first group belong the fleas already mentioned and also a kind of blowfly, whose maggots suck the blood of the young birds. If we had chosen to examine a house-martin's nest instead of a sparrow's, we should have found two more interesting parasites: a wingless fly related to the well known sheep-ked and a bug similar to the notorious bed-bug. This bug may invade our homes and make us painfully aware of its presence. The second group, the scavengers, includes all the insects described above, except the fleas, and many others which are less familiar. In addition to the two main groups, there are the insects which feed on the parasites and scavengers. They may be external carnivores, attacking their prey in a normal manner, or internal carnivores, which live and feed within the bodies of their victims.

If, before we throw away the remains of our sparrow's nest, we take a little of the fine dust and look at it through a microscope, we shall become aware of another population in the nest – a population of mites which, like the insects, can be divided into parasite and scavenger, hunter and hunted; but that is another story.

There is no need to try to stop birds from nesting on houses, except perhaps sparrows. If a nest is removed as soon as the last brood has flown the birds are obliged to build a new and clean one in the following spring, and it is unlikely that this will contain large numbers of insect pests until the autumn, when it can again be removed without discouraging the birds.

IN A GARDEN NEAR PARIS

Last spring a pair of black redstarts built their nest under the eaves of my house in a little box that I had put there for the purpose. When the nest was completed and the eggs laid, all was peaceful and the cock sang continuously in a nearby tree. Then something went wrong. New materials were brought to the box, in all haste it seemed to me, and for several days the birds were very busy. I dared not go up to investigate, for I did not want to add to their troubles. Then peace returned and the male resumed his singing, but with some dissonances due perhaps to the excitement caused by recent events. One morning, while both birds were away, I climbed up a ladder to find out what had happened. To my surprise I found two nests side by side. The eggs had been moved into the second which had been built since my previous investigation two weeks earlier. All that remained in the old nest was a large snail, five times the size of an egg, which was anchored right in the middle so firmly that part of the nest came away when I removed it. It had evidently climbed the wall to shelter from the hot sun and made it quite impossible for the hen to continue to sit on her eggs. She and her mate had built another nest in the box, and moved the eggs to it.

Guy M. Moreau, France

Camouflage: *Above*, a nightjar broods her young. *Below*, a cock reed-bunting mystified at finding the nest empty

A day-old swift takes food from its parent

Trying to brood a nestful of chicks, eleven days old, is a problem

At twenty days the young swifts are at the gawky stage

Now they are thirty-one days old and ready to fly

A sand-martin returns to her nearly fledged nestlings

More! More! Young swallows clamour for their meal

'Ware Baby-snatching

by Len Howard

EVERY nesting season I am besieged by people in search of advice on rearing young birds they have picked up, thinking this a kindness. They are surprised when I tell them that they have committed the crime of baby-snatching and must at once replace the fledglings where they found them, as only the parents can rear them successfully. These people, some of them children, imagine that a newly fledged bird will benefit from being shut indoors, away from cats, and fed on human diet with an occasional worm. This unnatural treatment would lead only to disaster, for even if the fledgling could be reared on such a diet, it would be unable to fend for itself when eventually set free.

There has been so much emphasis on 'instinct' in birds that it is often not realized that fledglings have to learn many things from their parents and from watching others of their kind. Their education begins in earnest directly they leave the nest, and in these early days most of them learn rapidly. If a fledgling is taken away from its natural surroundings and deprived of this essential training, it will not be alert for the dangers it will encounter when given freedom and, while making its first efforts to find food, may be taken unawares by a cat or other predator.

Often it is late afternoon when these young birds are picked up. Perhaps they appear deserted at that time because they need less food and their parents then take a rest, preen themselves and have a bathe. The parents also take time off around midday but usually keep within earshot of their young; if any predator appears they give alarm notes and make sure that the young take cover. On such occasions I have seen great tits kick or push their fledglings from exposed perches when the warning notes have not been heeded; they get taps on the head, too, if they utter cries before the danger is past. After the rest period the parents go food-hunting again but are often afraid to feed their young if people are watching them closely, so it is better not to remain near fledglings.

Sometimes people tell me they had to pick up the baby bird because it was crying and seemed deserted, but cases of desertion are rare. It is necessary and natural for young birds to cry; otherwise parents would have difficulty in finding all their offspring when these are scattered over their territory. When a fledgling has moved from its former perch and is under cover and silent, the father or mother arriving with food first adopts a listening pose with head erect. If the fledgling remains quiet the parent utters a special call-note which brings an answering cry, but usually, if it sees its parent coming with food, it cries of its own accord.

It is very rare for both parents to be dead. Even if there is definite evidence of this the fledglings should not be taken indoors. They have a chance of being adopted by another parent bird, so food should be given to them outdoors. If a young bird continues to cry, it may get food from one of its own species or even from another species. Last summer a hen blackbird came to my garden with an adopted song thrush. The first I saw of them was when the blackbird seized an outsize lump of bread from the young thrush's beak as it was struggling to swallow it. At first I thought this was a brazen case of theft, then the blackbird rubbed the bread on the ground to break it and returned it to the thrush's beak. It was late in the nesting season, and this foster-mother, half in moult, looked odd with ragged plumage and an upturned stump for a tail. The little thrush looked a dainty changeling beside her.

Brush was not one of my blackbirds, but they allowed this strange couple in their territory without dispute, for they had nearly finished nesting. Whenever Dainty cried, Brush snatched food from the lawn or from me and ran full tilt towards her adopted chick, which usually kept under cover of the flower borders, for Brush always travelled on foot; her wings were apparently weakened by moult and perhaps she had lost feathers in earlier disputes with rivals. She had no offspring of her own and all her attention was lavished on this youngster. It seemed that Brush was jealous of my feeding it, for when she saw Dainty taking food from me she came running up as fast as her legs would carry her.

She seized several pieces of food, which she hurriedly stuffed down the thrush's throat till it could eat no more. After disgorging, it tried to move away from the over-attentive foster-mother, but she pressingly pursued Dainty with more beakloads even when the food had been refused many times. She naturally did not realize that a young song thrush usually eats less than a young blackbird.

Sometimes people mistake a fledgling blackbird for a thrush, but they are not really alike. The former is dark brown above with a mottled brown breast, while the latter has a creamy-white breast with dark brown spots, the upper parts being a much paler brown.

Dainty showed much excitement on first finding a snail, but breaking the shell proved a problem for this young thrush, whose foster-mother preferred slugs, as do most blackbirds. After running round the lawn with the snail and occasionally dropping it on the grass, Dainty began tapping it hesitantly on the soft turf, then more sharply, but the shell did not break until eventually the youngster tried the concrete pathway with quick success.

A young bird's first attempts to feed itself are often amusing to watch. Last year a baby great tit happened to perch beside a large caterpillar which was crawling along the bough. The tit had never fed itself before, and this was big game which needed some handling. Cautiously the little tit hopped around the caterpillar, alternately bending low for close inspection and drawing back from nervousness; then quickly seizing it by the head, the tit darted up and down the bough with it dangling from a high-held beak. How to eat it was the problem, for parent tits always hold one end of a caterpillar firmly while their fledglings pull at the other end. At last the young tit stood still and, leaning forward, carefully hung the caterpillar round a small upstanding twig, half an inch high, then gave one end a pull. The result was disappointing and the caterpillar again dangled from the tit's beak, but another even more careful attempt was made to loop it firmly round the twig. Unfortunately this clever idea did not bring success to the young inventor, who soon left

37

the useless twig and held the caterpillar down with one foot, nearly losing balance with each pull while eating it. The experienced tit takes this food to a narrow perch, shaped so that the toes can grip while eating it.

So far tits have not been among the many species of young birds brought me; they are too active to be easily caught. A spotted flycatcher was picked up by a boy during the wet summer of 1957. He was astonished when I told him that flies were the food for his fledgling and that only the parents could rear it. This sort of interference is generally well meant, which makes it even sadder that so many birds perish through it. School teachers could be of great help if each spring they would give a talk about fledglings, explaining why interference is disastrous to them.

There is much need for such instruction. Judging from my experience, which includes numerous letters asking for advice, dozens of people must be taking fledglings away from their parents every nesting season and, entirely through ignorance, causing much loss of bird life.

SHARED NEST

For some years a blackbird or thrush nested in honeysuckle against a shed in my garden and reared a family; and on several occasions both nested peacefully side by side. Last year, a day or two after a thrush had begun to build, I heard a deal of commotion and saw a blackbird trying to drive it away. The contest was indecisive, and eventually the squabbling died down. Later the blackbird was seen bringing material to the nest the thrush had started, and the building was continued by both. The lining was left to the blackbird, the thrush giving up any attempt to finish the nest with mud. Soon after the thrush had laid two eggs the blackbird took a turn, though the thrush was back again the same day. When later I looked in the nest it contained two eggs of each; but this seemed to finish the joint effort, for both then deserted.

H. J. Morse, Wilts

Home-made Bird Tables

by E. M. Barraud

I HAVE seen many kinds of bird-table furniture and feeding gadgets in the gardens of friends, from the simplest tit-bells to elaborate contraptions more likely to snare birds than serve their needs, but I have had some fault to find with them all, apart from their cost. So I roughed out some ideas on paper, and on the next wet morning fetched from the wood-stack a length of elder stem which I had stood there after hedge-trimming in the early autumn. I cut four $3\frac{1}{2}$ inch lengths out of the stem where it was about $2\frac{1}{4}$ inches across, enlarged the centres with a screw-driver (not wishing to risk a chisel in the still sticky sap) till the rims were less than $\frac{1}{2}$ inch thick, and screwed an eyelet half-way along one side of each length. In half an hour I had four simple but effective logs for melted fat.

Next I made a tit-bell, which was just another length from the same elder stem. I fitted over one end a square of thin wood with an eyelet in it, and drilled a hole through both sides at the other end, about $\frac{1}{2}$ inch from its rim, slipping a small stick through as a perch. Any scrapings of fat can be melted down and poured into the log or bell, into which crumbs of bread, stale cake, potato and so on have already been pressed; the fat solidifies immediately and holds these fast. A log must be stood on a saucer or plate before it is filled, but very little fat soaks through the crumby mass.

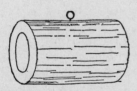

Birds love pecking at bones and pieces of bacon rind, but unless these are put in a holder of some sort the bigger and greedier birds get away with the lot; so next I made two holders for them. The first was inspired by a small wooden disc, about 2½ inches in diameter, which happened to be in the shed, but a square piece would have done equally well. I formed a little piece of wire netting – ½-inch mesh is the largest one should use – into a tube 4½ inches high, joining the two ends by twisting the wires together, and stapled it to the disc. Then I turned over the top edge neatly, fitted three bits of wire to the rim and linked them in an S-hook. Any scraps of food or bones are dropped in at the top, and the birds can easily get at them through the mesh.

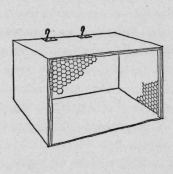

I elaborated on this for the second holder and it was worth the trouble, because the food is kept dry. I had a wooden box, quite rough, some 3 inches square and 6 inches long. First I hinged the lid to the box, and then knocked out two adjoining sides, which I replaced with small-mesh wire netting. (I did the hinging first as the box was firmer when it was whole.) Finally I put two eyelet-screws by the hinges. I now had a roofed feeder with two sides of wood and two of wire. When it is hung up, scraps can be placed in it by lifting the lid, and they fall against the wire where the birds can readily get at them.

Before I am asked how I find food enough for four logs, a tit-bell and two wire cages, I hasten to add that I gave away three of the logs, which are doing splendid service in the gardens of friends. The remaining log, bell and the wire cages I hung on my bird-table. This, too, is my own invention. The stem is a rough and forked branch of a tree, some 6 feet in length, and there is a tray with a rim on three sides, round the stem just where it forks. Originally I fixed it in the ground, but it interfered with lawn-mowing, so I made a tripod stand and the table is now portable and much handier. The tray, by the way, measures approximately 2 feet in length and is about 18 inches across; it has no roof, though this is often recommended, because I find birds do not like one, and a bird-table properly cared for will be kept clear of snow in bad weather, so that no roof is necessary. But birds do like the branches above the tray, and it is to these that I have attached the tit-bell and one wire feeder. The log and the other wire feeder hang from the corners of the tray. Just one thing more: I knocked two 3-inch French nails into the top of the tray, and over these I can press an occasional soft apple or any other food that needs an anchor.

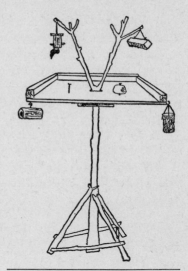

The bird-table may seem to be over-furnished, but usually every article is occupied and their multiplicity does save queueing and fighting. If the number must be reduced, I recommend jettisoning the box with the hinged lid and the tit-bell, not the open wire cage and the fat log. Of course, any of the four feeding aids may be hung on its own from a large gate-hinge screwed to a window-frame. This will appeal particularly to invalid or house-bound bird-watchers who like to see birds close to their windows.

MUSICAL SPARROW

A cock sparrow used to come regularly to our window to be fed and would tap on it if its meal was overdue. Afterwards it would sit on the bottom bar of the open window, usually when there was music on the radio. In the end we concluded that it liked to hear the music.

P. Simmons, Essex

WORKSHOP NEST

by D. E. R. Jeffery

To build her nest on the box marked 040 on the shelf at the right-hand side of the photograph, within arm's reach of where I stand in my workshop, a robin brought material in by the door and flew past my knees, or even between my feet, up to a perch behind me; she then flew to a shelf at my elbow and finally into the corner. On the return journey she went straight past my face to the door, and in thirty seconds she was back with moss. I watched her at close range and uncovered a broken window so that I could shut the door to keep cats away. She completed the nest in two days, after which I did not see her for a week. By April 2 there were three eggs, which hatched on the 25th.

On May 1 the bird's friendliness ceased and I was kept at a distance of 4 feet. The first time her wings brushed my face I thought it was an accident, but within two minutes my spectacles were nearly knocked off. I was attacked at least a dozen times during the morning, though only once was I testing the defence, when I moved towards the nest while the bird was on the trellis just outside; she had cleared the broken window and was beating against my face before I could move back. The cock would never approach the nest when I was on the scene, but when the hen flew to a branch of an apple tree and whistled he immediately appeared with food, with which she returned in a matter of seconds. The fledglings left on May 9, and four days later the nest was relined. On May 22 there were five more eggs, but tragedy overtook the hen after they were hatched, and her very nervous mate had to rear the larger family unaided. This he did successfully.

TASTE FOR PUTTY

Early last nesting season I was surprised to see that the putty was disappearing from the frame of our kitchen window. It was not long before I discovered that a blue tit which was nesting near by came to the window, pecked at the putty with violent blows and ate it. After many hours of waiting I managed to take the flashlight picture of it in the act. The putty had been left unpainted when the window was reglazed a short time previously.

Mark H. Waddicor, Surrey

HOMES FOR STARLINGS

On a visit to Moscow I noticed no starlings, though these birds are common enough in Russia. Can the reason be that they are adequately housed in the countryside? In the belief that they bring luck, the peasants erect boxes for them on long poles. I took the photograph in a west Russian village near Smolensk.

A. Nove, London

The robin bringing food to her nest in the box on the shelf at the right
Below, a blue tit caught in the act of eating putty from a window frame
Right, nest-boxes for starlings in Russia

The owl watched us quite unafraid

The Peace Offering

by Kenneth Richmond

W HEN Dougald telephoned to say that an owl was nesting in one of his outbuildings I was not enthusiastic. From his description it was undoubtedly a common-or-garden tawny owl. Still, it did seem to have chosen a rather unusual site and I promised to drive over.

For once I found Dougald at home. The owl too was there, squinting at us from a wooden box nailed in position about 5 feet from the ground in a corner of an open shed. Close by, in another box, an old hen sat quietly clucking to herself; and in the yard were black leghorns and speckled bantams. Immediately beneath the owl was a pile of coke for the greenhouse and a wheelbarrow with a sheep-dog asleep in it. The owl continued to watch us through the slits of her eyes, obviously quite unafraid though we were standing not more than 10 feet away. Then some incautious movement disturbed her, for her eyes opened and, brushing my shoulder, she made off to the wood. In the box lay four white eggs; not a trace of nesting material had been added to the layer of straw originally provided. I did not want to keep the bird away longer than was necessary and suggested that we should make ourselves scarce, but Dougald was in no hurry to move.

'Och, she's no' the one to be caring,' he said. 'Many's the day I've shovelled coke under her very nose and her not batting an eyelid. She'll be back in a minute.' And, as if to prove his point, the owl came wafting in as he spoke. For a moment she settled in the box, looking at us full-face, then slipped out again without a sound.

A fortnight passed and the first wheatears had arrived before I saw Dougald again. His farmyard was now swarming with day-old chicks.

'I'm thinking I'll have to tak' the gun to her,' he said. 'She's aye sitting there glowering at ma wee chicks. She'll be doing mischief amang 'em.'

I explained that it was most unusual for any bird of prey to kill in the immediate vicinity of its nest. I extolled the virtues of owls and appealed to his sense of justice by urging the need for presuming the bird's innocence until her guilt could be proved. But Dougald was obviously far from convinced.

'She's got claws, hasn't she?' he asked.

'Give her a chance for another week,' I pleaded, 'and I'll pay you a couple of bob for every chick she takes – if she takes any.'

'Aha, now ye're talking business,' he laughed, and we shook hands on the bargain.

When I arrived the following Saturday Dougald thrust a piece of paper into my hand. On it I read the fatal indictment: '3 Wyandotte chicks at 2*s*. each – 6*s*.'

'Wait till ye get the bill at the end o' the month,' he added sourly.

It began to look as though my liabilities might be heavier than I had bargained for.

'Are you sure it's the owl?' I asked. 'Have you actually seen her take one?'

'Och, it's no' herself's to blame,' he answered. 'More likely her auld man. He's sitting up in the tree yonder on the look-out.'

There was nothing for it but to pay up. Apparently I had backed a loser. Even so, I insisted on holding my friend to his bargain for another week. The case was still not proven.

On my next visit three more chicks were reported missing. Dougald was for taking the law into his own hands, and it seemed that no power of persuasion of mine would restrain him. Then, as we were discussing the affair, there was a scuffle in the yard and sudden outcry among the hens. Glancing sideways I saw a wee slip of a creature race along the side of the stables and dart into a hole in the wall – a weasel. In a moment it was out again, carrying something in its mouth. Dougald let fly with his stick as it dodged behind the wood-pile, the dog tried to grab it and in a twinkling the fugitive had made its getaway through a crack in the masonry. On the ground lay the bundle that it had been carrying – a dead chick. Dougald's suspicions were still far from being allayed, but the discovery of a second suspect stayed his hand, temporarily at least. I was relieved to think that my faith in the bird might not cost me anything after all.

When I next saw my friend he looked decidedly sheepish. He had a confession to make. The day before two more chicks had disappeared and he had fetched his gun. There seemed to be only one way of deciding once and for all whether the culprit was furred or feathered. In his eyes both were vermin, and the owl was a sitting target. The temptation had apparently been too great.

'So you got rid of her after all,' I said, disappointed.

'Guid sakes, no. Tak' a look for yourself, man,' he replied, beckoning me towards the open shed.

Sure enough the owl was installed in her usual place. As I went over, she flapped out into the sunlight and four wizened, gnomish faces reared up from the floor of the box. Stretched out beside them in the straw lay a scrap of fur, the limp and lifeless form of a weasel. I picked it up. Apart from two pinpoints of blood on the scruff of its neck where the owl's talons had transfixed it, there was little to show how the tiny beast had met its death. I turned and looked at Dougald.

'Dinna say it, dinna say it,' he protested. There was no point in rubbing it in.

'I'm thinking,' I said, 'that some folk are mighty hard to convince. It's almost as though she knew what was in your mind. A sort of peace offering, isn't it?'

'Aye, ye might call it that,' he agreed, grinning from ear to ear.

Dusk   This is the owl moment I have always known,
Not yet completely dark,
When small birds twit him in the park
In terror though they tease.
Out he comes among the trees,
He comes on oiled wings, alone,
And mice and tucked-up children hear
His long to-whooo as old as fear.

Frances Cornford

47

The Hoarders

by T. J. Richards

THAT certain animals conceal food is proverbial, but the extent to which birds possess the habit is not generally realized, and information on the subject is scanty. One of the most notable hoarders is the coal-tit. From the middle of September and throughout the autumn, parties of these tits are busily engaged in carrying away and hiding beechnuts. They conceal each nut in a different spot, so that the food supply may be dispersed over an area of up to a hundred yards from its source. One bird flies to a larch and thrusts the nut under a tuft of lichen. Another drops to a bank, pushes the nut into the earth and, after tapping it in, rearranges the moss. A third carries the nut to the mossy trunk of an oak, taps it into a bark-crevice and then cunningly conceals it with tufts of green moss. Where beeches grow at the edge of a pine-wood most of the nuts are hidden about the conifers or on the ground, under pine-needles and bracken. Coal-tits will hide food even in June – usually the seeds of Scots pines.

One or two nuthatches often work with the coal-tits, for they have an equally provident turn of mind. Their methods and places of concealment are similar, and they almost invariably cover the nuts with the material nearest to hand; a nuthatch that deposited food in a cavity in the bare trunk of a dead tree used chips and wood dust. One morning in May a cock nuthatch, which had been feeding his mate with insects as she sat on her eggs, arrived with an old hazel-nut in his beak. It seemed to occur to him, on reaching the vicinity of the nest-hole, that his offering was unsuitable for the occasion, because he flew to the stem of an ash tree and inserted the nut into a small round hole, which he then plugged with a tuft of lichen. Sometimes a nut or acorn may be broken up and partly eaten, and the remaining pieces hidden.

Marsh-tits also conceal food: beech-mast chiefly, but probably hazel-nuts as well. On a November day, when there were few nuts left on the trees and the birds were foraging on the ground, a marsh-tit found and secreted on a nearby bank thirteen beech-nuts in succession. The fourteenth it took to a branch and ate – an excusable lapse. While blue and great tits are usually in the party, they do not appear to conceal food. On several occasions I have observed great tits flying to spots where other birds had previously hidden nuts, but they have usually retired baffled. The great tit is something of a drone, for it stores no food itself, but keeps company with birds that do, and so benefits by their industry.

In country towns and villages where beech trees beautify gardens the birds hide nuts about flower-borders and shrubberies, and in niches of old walls.

Among the crow family, only rooks and jays hide food on anything like the same scale as tits and nuthatches. In early autumn parties of rooks begin to frequent the oaks, fluttering awkwardly on the outer sprays to pluck the ripening acorns; but close observation shows that they are not eating the fruit. They carry it away and bury it. The rook's methods are those of a true planter. It alights in a meadow and walks about with the acorn in search of the right place to bury it. Suddenly it pauses, tosses the acorn aside and proceeds to dig a hole with its pick-like bill. It then drops the acorn into the hole, taps it home and covers it up. Occasionally the bird buries an acorn several times before the job is completed to its satisfaction. Rooks will work thus for a considerable time; yet a subsequent examination of the field will reveal no sign of their labour.

Sometimes rooks may bury acorns a mile or more from the parent tree. Recently, in Devon, I watched individual birds take them from one valley to the next. As the crow flies the distance was about a mile, but as these rooks flew it was considerably farther. Instead of labouring over the hill, they flew down the valley for about half a mile until they reached the sea-cliffs. Then, utilizing upward air-currents, they drifted along the coast to the next valley where they turned inland and glided down to the fields. Two-thirds of their journey was accomplished with hardly a flap of the wing. On this occasion most of the birds carried a second acorn in the food-pouch.

How much of this concealed food is recovered and consumed? I would say the greater part of it; although I do not suggest that birds remember the hiding places. It is not necessary that they should. The food has been widely distributed over areas where they habitually forage during winter. Parties of tits and nuthatches haunt the same trees almost daily, tirelessly examining trunks, twigs and branches, flaking off bark, moss and lichen. Little escapes their sharp eyes and bills. They certainly find the nuts, sometimes only to hide them again in different places, and they continue to find them until May or June. Rooks, too, as they prod about in the fields, must unearth a considerable proportion of their hidden store.

Like the nuthatch, the great spotted woodpecker fixes galls and nuts in bark-crevices, so that it can hack them to pieces; but at times it will insert them and leave them untouched. Later they may be found by accident and consumed. Have we here the habit in its elementary stage? Perhaps in the course of time, if the custom be advantageous to the species, this woodpecker may learn to conceal its surplus food.

AFTER THE MEAL

In Vincent Square, London, pigeons had pecked the crumb out of slices of bread, leaving frames of crust. First one bird, then another manœuvred one of these over its head with its bill until it was wearing the crust as a necklace. One which managed to get two more round its neck walked over and displayed, bowing and head-bobbing, to another pigeon.

I watched this curious behaviour for quite ten minutes, during which time the three-necklet bird lost two crusts, picked them up and got them over its head again with a tossing movement of the bill. When the pigeons were finally alarmed by a dog and flew off, one was still carrying a crust of bread round the base of its neck. *G. M. Clayden, Cornwall*

PIGEON COMPANIONS

When I was a boy, my mother was given a pair of Indian lotan pigeons – handsome birds with pure white plumage, pink feet and legs, and glorious ruby-coloured eyes. My brother and I volunteered to look after them and put them in a loft over the stables. They soon began to follow us wherever we went, and were not long in discovering our bedroom window. In one corner of the room was an antique wardrobe with a wide carved frame round the top, about 9 inches from the ceiling, to which they brought sticks; then two eggs were laid. The cock bird roosted on the frame overlooking the nest, and every morning as soon as it got light he would fly down on to the bottom of the bed and walk up to where we were sleeping. If neither of us was awake he would pull our hair. This meant that the window had to be opened wide. He would then fly on to the sill, and to this day I can hear the crack of his wings as he took off. He used to come back promptly at 10 a.m. and take his turn sitting till 4 p.m., when the hen returned. Our secret was not discovered until two broods had been reared.

Cecil B. Barrow, Derbyshire

RETRIBUTION

Our homestead is one of the oldest in this part of New South Wales, with dining-room, kitchen and men's mess-room separated from the other rooms by a boarded walk which has a rounded iron roof about 60 yards long. One morning from the dining-room window my husband and I were watching our old cat Nigger walk sedately along this roof trying to keep his balance, when a wagtail began to dive-bomb him at intervals and peck at his head and neck. Eventually the bird sat on Nigger's back for the rest of the trip, evidently aware that he could not lift a paw without losing his balance. The wagtail was one of a pair building a nest in the pepper tree overhanging the garden path. Each time I went to the gate under the tree it would swoop down and peck at my hand, taking away hairs for its nest.

Jean Hunt, New South Wales

DECEMBER STARLINGS

At the end of a warm, sunny October we saw a pair of starlings come with nesting material to a hole caused by a broken tile near our bedroom chimney. By the middle of November we saw only one bird going in and out. Not until December was their brood hatched, and they worked at top speed to ensure its survival. As we never get more than a taste of our cherries, starlings do not head the list of our many feathered friends, but we felt that this event deserved its reward and did not replace the tile.

Evelyn Richardson, Kent

Birds and Lighthouses   *by Richard Fitter*

IN the early years of this century immense numbers of small birds were being killed against lighthouses, especially those with revolving white lights. Before the light of the Galloper lightship, beyond the Thames estuary, was altered from white to red, the keepers returning from duty used to take ashore clothes-baskets full of larks, though no migrants approached the light after the change. At the Skaw lighthouse, on the other hand, there was a substantial increase in the number of birds attracted to the light when it was changed from a fixed to a revolving one: on a single October night a thousand were dashed to death.

One of the first effective pieces of positive bird protection in Britain was the erection of perches at selected lighthouses by the Royal Society for the Protection of Birds so that tired migrants could alight and roost instead of fluttering blindly round the light. At present four lighthouses – Bardsey, the Skerries, the South Bishop and St Catherine's (Isle of Wight) – are so equipped at migration seasons; but the perches may soon be replaced by flood-lighting, which is cheaper and more effective.

After its very successful experience with electric flood-lighting at Dungeness, the Society seems likely to go over completely to flood-lighting, electric on the mainland and paraffin on islands. Paraffin flood-lights are already installed on Flatholm in the Bristol Channel and at the Longstone, Grace Darling's famous lighthouse on the Farnes off the coast of Northumberland. They are less powerful than the electric but quite adequate to light up a 120 foot tower from the ground. An unexpected result of flood-lighting is that many birds fly lower round the tower and so are kept out of the lighthouse's main beam, which would dazzle them. Several other lighthouses need flood-lighting in addition to the four which now have perches. A few years ago I saw dead starlings, redwings and song thrushes under Strumble Head light on the coast of Pembrokeshire. The photograph shows warblers found by a relief keeper, G. J. Evans, on the gallery rail of the Hanois lighthouse off the southern tip of Guernsey. One morning in the autumn of 1956 he found as many as seventy dead or dying there.

Perches for migrant birds
at St Catherine's Lighthouse

Below, dead flycatchers on the
gallery rail of the Hanois
lighthouse

A long-eared bat wakes from his upside-down sleep, climbs grotesquely on top of a wall, takes off – and is away in swift, effortless flight on its night's hunting

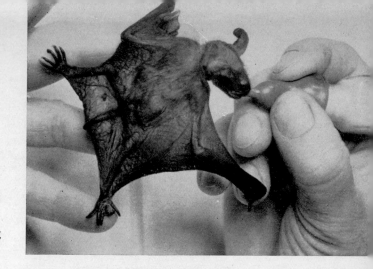

A mouse-eared bat,
one month old, feeding
from a doll's bottle

The baby bat clings
with its thumb-claws

Both bats showed the
greatest eagerness to
climb on to the hand
that fed them

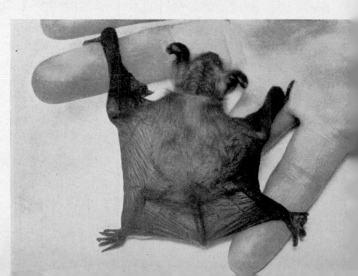

Bats on the Bottle

by Jean McDougall

IN the first days of June 1953 zoologists from Basle University found a colony of mouse-eared bats hanging in clusters from the beams of an old church. They were mothers with new-born young clinging to their fur, and a few were taken for observation to the Zoology Department, where they were fed for several weeks on meal-worms. When I first saw them in their large cage the young ones were from four to eight days old, still blind and hairless. The adult bats were hanging quietly in one corner of the cage, covering with their wings the babies which clung to them. One baby whose mother had died was hanging from the roof. Another had fallen to the floor and had been bitten in the foot when an attempt was made to hang it on to its mother again.

These two baby bats were squeaking desperately as they cast their heads from side to side in search of milk, and I asked whether they could not be reared by hand. My zoologist friends thought that they were too young, but instructed me in the art of dipping a small piece of sponge into warm milk and trying to get it into the baby bat's mouth. They did not know what food to give them nor how often, so I had to experiment.

I wrapped the small naked youngsters in cotton-wool and set off to the nearest dairy to buy a bottle of pasteurized milk. It was curious how the other people in the shop, and afterwards in the tram, did not notice the urgent high-pitched squeaks coming from my open handbag. Whenever they stopped, I feared they had died, but when I got home and unwrapped the two bundles the squeaking became louder, and two dark heads with big papery ears were weaving desperately on the thin necks, searching for their mothers' furry bodies and the life-giving milk. They looked like skinny fragile little dragons with wings hanging like limp cloth and open mouths framed with tiny pin-point teeth.

The smaller of the two, which had been bitten in the foot, had been without its mother's milk for more than twenty-four hours and was in a bad way, so that its chances of survival seemed extremely slender. It was unable to use the injured foot to crawl, and its sounds were much fainter than the piercing cries of the bigger one. I took it in my hand and dipped the pointed piece of sponge into the warm milk. When its mouth opened to squeak, I pushed the tip of the sponge in and then tried to squeeze milk along it. Usually the little creature bit on the sponge too hard in its eagerness to get more, and the milk flowed into its nostrils, which are inconveniently near the lips of baby bats. Then I had to dry it with a paper handkerchief and start the whole manœuvre again. After we had both worked hard for about half an hour the little animal had had enough milk to quieten it.

The bigger bat, which may have been a few days older, was much more vigorous and could crawl on my hand, using its two feet and wrists. It did not take well to the sponge method of feeding, so I tried a fine glass pipette, the top of which I had to force gently between its closed lips before slowly running in some milk. After a few days I discovered that a doll's feeding bottle with rubber teat was far more convenient.

On the first day I fed the bats every two hours and gave the last feed at midnight, when I set the alarm for four o'clock. I had wrapped them in paper handkerchiefs (cotton-wool caught on their claws and teeth) and put them in a cardboard box with a warm rubber water-bottle under it. I did not expect the smaller one to survive the night, but when I picked up the little paper sausage in the morning, a weak but urgent squeaking greeted me. The bat sucked at the sponge, and I noticed that I could watch the stomach fill with milk through the transparent skin of its hairless belly. This became a useful means of knowing when to stop feeding, for sometimes the stomach would swell alarmingly. I could also see how often the stomach became empty, and was able, after a few days, to cut down the number of meals to four and later to three a day.

For three days I kept both bats rolled in paper handkerchiefs. Then I decided that the bigger one might be better hanging upside down, as in the natural state. At first the babies are carried everywhere on their mothers' bodies, clinging to their fur as they hang upside down all the day and as they fly out at night to catch insects. After a week or so the young ones are left behind when the mothers fly out, and hang alone.

I therefore hung the larger bat by its toes on a twig pushed through the upper part of an up-ended boot-box, and there it stayed for hours without the slightest difficulty. The very sharp claws on the toes give a grip on any slightly rough surface. Later I attached a piece of an old fur collar to the twig, so that the youngster could, if it wished, hold on the furry surface with its thumb claws, as well as hang by its toes. Although this fur may have been a mechanical help, I do not think that it became a true 'mother-substitute', for both young bats always showed the greatest eagerness to climb off their perch on to my hand, even when they were not hungry. After a feed they seemed to be quite content hanging by their toe-nails from one of my fingers with their bodies pressed against the warmth of my palm. They would squeak when lifted off again to be returned to their perch with the fur.

After a week, when its damaged leg had quite healed, the weaker bat was strong enough to hang beside the bigger one. Nevertheless, it always seemed more nervous of falling than the other.

The bigger bat now began to develop a certain nonchalance. It would hang by one foot and use the other to scratch itself all over, twisting about to reach behind its head and into its paper-thin ears. One evening it hung by one foot from my finger, curled into a ball, and began to clean its wings thoroughly and systematically. For twenty minutes it worked away industriously, passing every bit of transparent silk-like wing through its mouth, licking it, stretching it and tugging at it energetically. After this tremendous effort it suddenly lay quite still in my hand, scarcely breathing, in the alarming way bats have.

At night-time both youngsters began to stretch out one wing to its full extent, tensing and shivering it for a few minutes before folding it again to stretch the other. Soft downy coats of brown hair had grown on their backs, and they had become very agile at climbing up the strip of fur to reach the hanging perch. Their eyes opened after a fortnight, and they seemed to keep healthy on a diet of pasteurized cow's milk thickened with human baby-food; every second day I added lemon juice for vitamin C, and a vitamin A and D concentrate.

No Trace of Fear

by Len Howard

ONE day when I was lying by the sea-shore in a Devon cove, a half-grown bank-vole came up to me. The first intimation of its arrival was the feel of its muzzle sniffing my arm; it then snuggled into the palm of my hand and seemed to like being stroked. When I lifted it close to my face it sat looking up at me without a trace of fear. It ate the cheese from my sandwiches with much relish, but refused the bread. This Tom Thumb creature, about two and a half inches long with a quarter of an inch of tail, was completely delightful in appearance and in its ways. Wondering if it could swim, I took it over the sands to a narrow pool about nine feet long. Directly I put it on the brink it shot down the whole length of the pool at lightning speed, keeping most of its body above water; then it landed and without hesitation ran back to me. I was so surprised at its immediate return that I repeated the experiment and it behaved in just the same way, except that it paused to shake itself after the swim and chose the other side of the pool for its run back. When I picked it up only its underparts were wet.

The voles in my garden would be tame if I did not have to discourage them; otherwise they come indoors. Sometimes when a bone which I have put out for the tits falls to the ground, a vole seizes its chance and lugs it, bit by bit, into the cover of leafage under the bird-table. The tits watch from a perch above, fidgeting uneasily. Harvest-mice and pigmy shrews also feed on the bones, but only the harvest-mice can reach those suspended on string. I have watched one run up the bird-table and along the twig to which the string was attached, then loop the tip of its tail round the twig and hang head downwards to feed. After I had removed the string and bones, this harvest-mouse ran along the twig to get another feed, knotting its tail round the twig as before and hanging where the bones had been. It sniffed and searched the air in a puzzled manner for a minute or two, then hauled itself up and ran back to the bird-table and down to the ground. No sooner had it touched earth than it turned round and ran back to the twig, repeating the plunge into space to search for the bones. It must have been able to see that they were not there, but it certainly did not believe its eyes, for it repeated the whole performance three times before it ran away.

One summer a pigmy shrew came into the kitchen and got inside the large cardboard carton in which the grocer had sent my provisions, including bacon bones wrapped in paper. The little creature tore off the wrapping and gnawed the bones, but left everything else in the carton untouched. After I had removed all the other provisions I found it again in the box, and now that the packages had gone it could not get out; its efforts to climb up the slippery surface of the glazed cardboard were as fruitless as those of a spider trapped in a bath. Unlike the patient spider, the pigmy panicked, rushing round the box, trying first one place, then another, and crying excitedly in a high-pitched voice. The rapid short sequences of notes were much more musical than the sounds other small animals can produce. The pigmy showed no fear at being lifted out; we were already familiar, for it had often come close to me in the garden. It used to open the tits' match-boxes, containing cheese, which I always have by me. Its long pointed snout seemed an efficient tool for this purpose, but it had difficulty in steadying the box and the performance was amusing to watch, for this shrew can show a lively impatience when it wants something. It can also be very obstinate, as I know to my cost.

One morning there were two pigmies in the carton, so I turned them out of the house, shut the bones in a cupboard and kept the kitchen door closed, having decided that pigmies must no longer be allowed indoors. The next morning I was about to push the carpet-sweeper along

a rug in the sitting-room when I heard squeaks of protest. Opening the sweeper, I saw one of the pigmies sitting in a corner of the dust-collector, staring up at me; and it refused to move. I shook and tapped the sweeper and tried both coaxing and scolding in strong language, for sweeping rugs was impossible with the creature inside. When I tried to lift it out, it dodged behind framework too narrow for my hands, so I took the sweeper up the garden and left it there, thinking that my efforts to expel the shrew would make it glad to take advantage of my absence to escape. Ten minutes later I returned to find it still sitting in the corner, and when I bent close, its eyes flashed at me as if in defiance. Was this, the smallest of all mammals, deliberately being obstinate, perhaps even taking pleasure in frustrating me? I seized the sweeper, turned it upside down and shook it roughly without result. Then I tried poking with a stick, but the pigmy dodged every poke with consummate skill, jumping from one part of the sweeper to another. In despair I fetched a cup of water, and when I splashed this inside, the shrew jumped out and ran into the the grass. My triumph was short-lived, however, for on the next and many later mornings I found it back in the same corner of the sweeper, which I had to take up the garden daily in order to remove the pigmy by splashing water over it. One day when I had got rid of the creature I found that the sweeper would not work, as it was clogged with rust. I feel that one meaning of the word 'shrew' must have arisen from embittered reactions to defeat in personal encounters with this animal. Incidentally, there seem to be varying accounts of its eyes; one book suggests that they see little except bright light and perhaps not even this, whereas another says that the eyes, though small, are well developed. The movements and actions of my pigmy showed that it had sight, and from the appearance of its eyes there was no reason to doubt this.

That same summer, drought had hardened the clay soil and the moles may have been having a lean time, for one came out of a tuft of grass in my orchard and burrowed its head inside a paper-bag containing cheese on the ground beside me.

I discourage long-tailed field-mice because they do so much harm, but they seem unafraid and sometimes perch on tall stems of hedge-parsley in my orchard, looking most handsome with their white underparts showing. Sometimes I see them with head stretched forward to reach the young seeds which they seem to like in their fresh green state. They can be very playful I have seen their riotous romping on the corrugated iron roof of a wooden hut where I lived for a year. Rats were there too, and the terrific noise made by their feet in their orgies on the roof used to keep me awake. They ignored my bangs on it from inside, and frequently I had to go out in the small hours to chase them away. On the moonlight nights the sight of them leaping and rushing round the roof was fantastic. During the day one or two rats often looked at me through the window, but the field-mice were more discreet.

Wild animals at play are always interesting. I have seen a weasel amusing itself by running up and then rolling down a steep bank about twenty feet high. At first I thought that it might have lost its balance unintentionally, for weasels cannot resist a sharp turn of the head to glance at an approaching human before they disappear from sight, and this might cause them to overbalance on a steep slope. This one, however, was too intent on its game to notice my presence, and the way it threw itself over convinced me that it wanted to roll down the bank.

THOSE EARS!

In frosty weather a young wild rabbit approached an Essex farmhouse and, being fed and encouraged, found his way into the kitchen. The cat, who was sitting on a rug by the fire, regarded him at first with wary astonishment, but before long proceeded to wash the trembling stranger. The two became friends, and the rabbit, though free to come and go as he pleased, spent most of his days with the cat in the warm kitchen. But she could not stand his habit of erecting his ears, which she smacked down so promptly that he got accustomed to keeping them down; when he did start to erect them he would remember and lower them quickly. Eventually, when summer came, he returned to the woods, where rabbits can wear their ears as they please.　　*Janet Norton, Sussex*

As a boy Mr Robertson Scott, the founder of *The Countryman*, had a long-eared rabbit which used to come into the kitchen and made friends with the cat. She used to take its ears between her paws and wash them carefully inside and out.

A mole enjoys a
worm before going
underground

'Shall I unroll? The danger seems to have gone'

A stretch, a roll over – and the young hedgehog crawls away

Hedgehogs in the Kitchen

by Joyce Averil

ONE year in October four young hedgehogs were found wandering in a garden on the edge of the Forest of Dean, whistling their urgent call for mother and food. They had been born too late in the season to hibernate, so that their only hope of survival was to be taken indoors for the winter. They seemed quite at home in the kitchen in a large box of hay and beech leaves, where they slept on top of each other, as they could not yet curl into tight balls. When offered milk from a pen-filler they refused it, preferring to tackle bread and milk, spluttering knee-deep in a saucer. They objected with much snuffling to scraped raw meat pressed against their noses, but then tore at it with tiny sharp teeth; thereafter they noisily champed up quantities of best lamb, liver and boiled cod, though wholemeal bread and milk remained their favourite meal.

I tried not to let them become too tame, as I did not intend to keep them indoors permanently. Nevertheless they tolerated handling, and only a sudden careless movement would make them hunch their shoulders and throw out their prickles in stiff array. By the end of November they had doubled their size, no longer sat in the middle of their saucer to feed and during the day slept as four separate spiny balls. Sounds of heavy breathing, like old-fashioned bellows, would come from their box, and expressive sizzling noises denoting excitement or slight resentment, often caused by the sudden entrance of one of the family into the nest. Occasionally this was followed by a low bubbling sound or a characteristic snuffling sneeze.

They soon discovered that they could push out of the side of their wire run. I nearly tripped over Whistle in the passage one evening. Another night Urchin explored the sitting-room and scattered the sticks and newspaper in the grate. Wuffles squeezed under the kitchen stove and remained there scrabbling and snuffling, in spite of all my efforts to pull her out. In the end I had to wait quietly until she emerged of her own accord. Then I caught her, and as I carried her back to the nursery she sneezed and pushed at my fingers with strong brown paws which felt like warm chamois leather. She was very pretty, her dense soft coat being a charming shade of silver-fawn with dark markings on each side of her face.

One night there were sounds as of a burglar who had found the home-made wine and was being careless with the bottles. At the top of the stairs I was met by an aromatic silence. When I switched on the kitchen light Urchin was sitting quite still under the table, and Whistle was curled up behind the coal box. Wiffles was on his way to the sitting-room. It was Wuffles who had squeezed into the cupboard under the stairs and played skittles with the lightly corked wine bottles. Two lay on their sides in a crimson pool of elderberry wine and there was a tell-tale track back to the box.

All four sometimes got up to mischief, but they spent a lot of time making their nest comfortable, pushing and scraping at the sawdust, which they piled up into the corners and all round themselves, filling in cracks and blocking out draughts. One evening they wrapped themselves in a whole sheet of newspaper and with noisy pulling, pushing and crumpling tore it into fragments. The result was so satisfactory that they invariably used their newspaper carpet when short of leaves.

THE PIPES OF PAN

For some days we had been puzzled by a high-pitched piping or whistling note in the garden. It was a peculiar, penetrating noise, that seemed to be everywhere. Late one evening, as I returned home in the dark, I heard it again, very insistent and seeming louder than ever in the silence of the night. By the time I had fetched a torch it had stopped.

Suddenly, right at my feet, the noise started again and the light of my torch showed a mother hedgehog having trouble with a young one, which apparently had fallen down the rockery wall and was unable to climb up again. It failed to get a firm grip on the stones, as its mother was able to do, and kept falling backwards. It had evidently grown too large for its mother to carry it in the usual manner, rolled up underneath her, although she tried several times. The only other way she could help was to push her nose under it, manœuvre it on to her back and give it a heave up the wall. Unfortunately, every time she lifted the young one, her spines stuck into its soft little belly and caused it to squeal. Knowing that the human voice can have a reassuring effect on animals I spoke softly to the mother, which stood calmly by, as I placed her offspring safely on top of the wall, where she immediately followed. The pair then walked off, the baby gambolling at the mother's side. Since that night there has been no more piping, so I can only conclude that the old hedgehog had been trying to get the young one up the rockery for several days.

Joan Blewitt Cox, Devon

MOUSE MYSTERY

I had had the experience of milk disappearing unaccountably, till one day I saw a mouse hanging down in a pint bottle, an inch of its tail hooked over the moulded top. Evidently it was able to draw itself out, for an hour or so later it had gone. After milk has been poured from a bottle some of it dries on the lip, leaving it less slippery. A mouse's tail is very muscular, of course: I have seen one drag a piece of bread by coiling its tail round it. *M. Wood, Lancs*

MOUSE LARDERS

For more than two weeks a field-mouse brought in alive by the cat was our unwanted guest, but not for several months after we had finally trapped it did we discover where it had made its home. Deciding that the furniture was wrongly placed, we moved the piano and there, neatly tucked into one of the joists at the back near the top, was a beautifully made nest. Strips had been torn from the material backing the instrument, and the nest lined with bits of wool and fluff from the rugs.

The *chef-d'œuvre* was the methodically arranged larder. Various foods were stored separately in compartments at the bottom of the piano: nuts in one, bread and cake crumbs in another, bacon rind in a third, and bits of chocolate and toffee in a fourth. It was a marvel of ingenuity.

Elizabeth Maitland, Hants

One evening, after an autumn gale, when my husband thought the hens had laid extra well, he realized that from one nest he was picking up more apples than eggs. He emptied the nest, throwing out 7 or 8 apples, but the next evening even more had been stored there. A day or two later there was quite half a pailful, mostly Ellison's Orange, about the size of a golf ball. A long-tailed field-mouse had gnawed a hole through the corner of the lean-to hen-house. It had had to raise the apples 3 inches.

Ann Totman, Oxon

A Troublesome Guest

by Harry Moorhouse

BEFORE I put away the ladder after picking the apples, I take
down the nest-boxes that were occupied during the summer and
empty out the contents. They usually contain large numbers of spiders and
earwigs, but last autumn I found a more interesting and unexpected
creature in a box in a tree near the house. As soon as I had climbed up
and grasped the box, a bewhiskered grey head appeared at the entrance
with an angry hissing sound. Thinking it was a rat, I hastily withdrew
my fingers and found something to put over the hole. Then I removed the
nest-box from the tree and shook its contents into a large wooden box.
Out of the mess of straw and feathers streaked a little creature about the
size of a half-grown rat, with a thick bushy tail like a squirrel's, and I
remembered the edible dormouse (*Glis glis*) reported in our district a
year or two ago. As a rule the thrill of seeing a new bird or animal in
the garden gives me more pleasure than keeping it as a pet. But here was
something unusual and I was tempted to keep it for a while in a glass-
fronted box in our living-room.

Originally a native of Mediterranean countries, the edible dormouse
was released in Tring Park about sixty years ago and has spread over the
surrounding country. Owing to its habit of entering the upper parts of
houses in search of shelter and food, it threatens to become a nuisance.
But its diet appears to be restricted to fruit, vegetables and nuts, and it is
undoubtedly a less objectionable and more cleanly creature than the
omnivorous rat. Indeed, the Romans are said to have kept large numbers
for eating: hence the name. It is an engaging little animal. Its body, grey
above and dirty white below, is some 5 inches long, and its bushy tail
about the same length. It resembles the grey squirrel in all but size,
although it is not so attractive in the face because its round naked ears

are more rat-like than the squirrel's. The large ears and eyes suggest nocturnal habits, and ours spent most of the day curled up asleep with the tip of its bushy tail across its forehead, as though to shield its eyes from the light. Its agility was remarkable. It could leap on to the smooth sides of its box and cling there with ease.

In a day or two Sammy, as ours was called by the children, lost a great deal of his wildness and ate heartily the acorns and apples provided. But one night he gnawed a hole through the back of his thin wooden box and disappeared. Next morning almost every part of the room revealed how he had enjoyed his freedom; curtains, bookshelves, picture-rail, piano, window-sills and mantelpiece had all been thoroughly explored. Most of the fruits, including some tomatoes in a bowl on the sideboard, had been sampled and he had feasted on sweet chestnuts.

As the door of the room had been open, there was a chance that he was at large in the house. Otherwise he could be hidden only in the chimney – a possibility also suggested by loose soot in the hearth. The fire was lit during the day and we hoped that, if he was there, he would have to climb to the top and leave the house that way. We saw and heard nothing of him before we went to bed that night, but we left an apple on the floor. Sooty footprints everywhere the next morning left no doubt that, in spite of the smoke and heat, he had hidden in the chimney. All that remained of the apple was the skin.

Each morning, after two more nights of freedom, we cleared up the mess. Then we decided that he must go. A trap was baited with an acorn and that was the end. We told ourselves that Sammy and his kind might one day become pests, like grey squirrels. All the same, we might have left him in the garden.

MICE AND STRAWBERRIES

I did not discover that mice eat strawberries until I put cardboard collars round each of my plants. One day I found several wet, pulpy berries, from which every seed had been removed (some were already mildewed), and here and there on the cardboard were tiny heaps of husks from the seeds. I suspected mice only when, later, I saw droppings in plenty on the cardboard. Traps gave me a mixed bag of long-tailed field-mice, voles and, more rarely, house-mice. *Campbell Keith, Dorset*

LEVERET IN RHODESIA by Ida Lapham

One of our native 'boys' brought us a leveret out of the veld. As I was busy, I put it temporarily into a box with a twist of hay in the dining-room, away from my two Scotties which chase hares in the veld with great enthusiasm. The box was quite 10 inches deep, and I thought that there was no possibility of such a small creature getting out of it, but in a few minutes I found it on a tour of inspection of the room. I put it back to see how it managed to get out. It sprang up, again and again, with a jack-in-the-box motion, a little higher each time, keeping in the middle of the box; then somehow it was suddenly balanced on its tummy on top of one side and flopped over to resume its inspection.

I made it a 'form' from an old woollen scarf and pressed it into this in the box, hoping that it would sleep. It did, and I admitted the Scotties with much misgiving, wondering if the smell would remind them of the many hares they chase and never catch. But they were enchanted with the leveret, and it with them; it did not show the slightest fear. They hung over its box like doting parents over an infant's cot, left their dinners half-eaten to return to it, and followed it about the room, sniffing, prodding and making ecstatic noises.

Feeding was a problem. Eventually we managed with a small ear-syringe, without its plunger and with a piece of valve-rubber on the point for a teat. But the leveret seemed all legs and jerks at feeding times, until I discovered that, if it was rolled (while in a crouching position) in a cloth into a tight little sausage, with only its mask showing – it was quite unmanageable if its ears were left out – it could be held in one hand for feeding, and sucked and guggled happily. We could lay it down afterwards like a tiny mummy, and it seemed to like this. It would sit in our hands and clean itself with something like passion. The last feed at nine o'clock interested the little animal most, and it knew the sounds of food-preparation in a house otherwise silent at that time. The first tinkle of a spoon brought its eager gaze.

But trouble lay ahead. The leveret bubbled and guggled the milk down its chest at every feed and the small black ants, of which we have millions, soon found it. There seemed to be no remedy. If we washed its neck and chest they were never dry. The ants became a torment, and we sadly decided that it was kindest to say good-bye to the little creature, which had been a charming pet for the ten days we had had it. And once more we said, 'Never again'.

Hetty the Hamster

by Phyllis K. Thorne

EVEN at six weeks old Hetty was a true golden hamster, self-possessed and very curious. Kipling's motto for the mongoose family, 'Run and find out', might well apply to this inquisitive little rodent whose chief joy is new ground to explore. Nocturnal and short-sighted, sensing her way with quivering nose and whiskers, Hetty will enter anything with confidence, never suspecting a trap. Her only nervousness is of wide open spaces, which she crosses quickly with ears flattened and *ventre à terre*. She prefers to run round the skirting and quickly forms a 'path habit' in each fresh room. This sometimes leads to trouble. When a piece of furniture was moved into her path she ran heavily into the legs.

In summer there are logs in the dining-room hearth – lovely things to nibble and explore. Hetty was soon at home there, including it in her scamper round the room, but when the first fire was lit in autumn she would have dashed straight into it, had I not been close enough to scoop her up, inches from the edge.

She can engage reverse gear easily – an advantage in her natural state as a burrowing animal. While her claws are not made for enlarging a burrow in hard ground, the speed with which she gets through soft earth suggests this as her habitat. She piles sawdust around her nest in the same manner: after scratching it together with her front paws she mounds it up behind with an energetic kick of the hind legs. Another indication of underground life is her determination to build her nest under the shelf in her cage. Once we moved this to the other end and she came out grumbling to investigate; then, with eyes half shut and ears squashed with sleep, she began immediately to move her entire bedding to shelter again – no small task.

Hetty will climb readily: bracing herself between furniture and wall she quickly reaches the top of the wardrobe and descends only a little less easily, head first. But she cannot climb squirrel fashion, for her paws are daintier and claws far less powerful. She can, however, make good use of individual claws by which to hang: one hooked in the wire-netting will momentarily take her full weight (5 oz. at six months old) while she feels around with her front feet for the next foothold. Her sense of direction is good. It was not long before she could find her way back from any upstairs room to the dining-room, and when her cage was moved to the top of the bookshelves for warmth she soon realized its new position and found a method of reaching it by scrambling up between the books.

Apart from the need for warmth and freedom from draughts, a golden hamster is an unexacting pet. Given water and a daily feed of greenstuff and dog-biscuit, with treats of nuts, a *glacé* cherry or a muscatel, it lives happily and rewards its owner with amusing demonstrations of its activities, not only in the unnatural surroundings of a house, but perhaps more when about its rightful business of nest-building, washing and feeding. The cheek pouches provided for carrying food to the burrow are a source of constant interest.

Hetty never fails to get a smile when she has filled up with several small nuts and, hurrying back, rattles alarmingly as she climbs the book-shelves to her larder.

MORE WAYS THAN ONE

A neighbour's sheepdog, trained to stop the flock on the road at a word of command, would jump the wall and run the other side of it to head them off. One day the flock filled a narrow road whose walls were too high to climb. When the order to stop them rang out the dog hesitated only a second; then, using the backs of the sheep as stepping-stones, he jumped from one to the next so swiftly and lightly that they showed no resentment, till he got ahead of them. Afterwards he always used this method at that part of the road.

E. D. Twiss, Sligo

Hetty the Hamster senses her way with quivering nose and whiskers and is afraid of nothing except wide open spaces

Over page, field-mice among the roots of trees

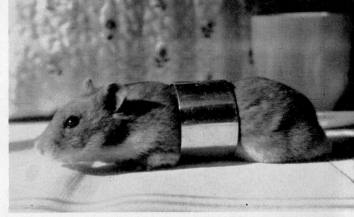

A **pine** marten's remarkable jump from pole to branch. He comes down head first

Ready for anything   Training a pine marten to follow a pan of food

My Pine Martens

by H. G. Hurrell

IT was in 1938 that I first acquired three pine martens which had been imported from Germany. I remember being impressed at once by their broad, rather flat heads and strong thick legs, with feet that leave tracks suggesting a larger animal.

I keep and breed the martens at my home on the southern fringe of Dartmoor in pens formerly used for silver foxes. They do not seem to be encumbered by their stout limbs, for they exercise themselves for hours and their movements are often very rapid. It is fascinating to watch the exciting chases of playful cubs rushing in wild pursuit from one end of their large pen to the other. Martens rarely walk; they normally progress by a succession of easy bounds with backs arched, thus showing their relationship to the weasel. They have a swinging rhythm, and I often picture them bounding through the forest like sprites. The names I give them – Zephyr, Ripple, Eddy, Swirl – suggest the movement which is their very essence.

A faulty door-catch allowed one of the two original males to escape. I hunted high and low but realized how hopeless it was to try to re-capture an animal which could easily climb the guard fence that had prevented the escape of my silver foxes. Imagine my surprise and delight the following day to see him run along a wall, flip over the fence and go straight back to his pen, where a feed was waiting. This experience with a marten which was not even bred in this country encouraged me to let one out deliberately. I had fearful qualms about losing it, but within a day or so it returned; and this led me to try to control a marten while out, so as to get it back at will.

I have had a lot of experience in training hawks, especially goshawks, and wondered if martens could be trained by an adaptation of the method. Hawks must first be accustomed to human beings; then they are trained to feed on a lure. As soon as they are tame and know that the lure means food, the main problem is to ensure that they are keen before being flown. For my martens I have invented a special kind of lure, a pan on a long handle: I cannot help calling it a martinet, though it is not a spur but an enticement. Food can be placed in the pan and the animal encouraged to eat from it. Eventually he is taught to follow the pan for a reward and so can be allowed a short distance from the pen and lured back there. The training may take some time but, as with hawks, it becomes mainly a matter of keeping the creature tame and seeing that it has a good healthy appetite when at liberty. By tame I mean willing to feed close to a human being; my martens would strongly object to being handled. The similarity of the response of hawk and marten is remarkable: if they are not keen they may go off on their own regardless of their owner and his lure. But there is one great difference. As a rule a hawk cannot be relied on to return home after it has been lost; eyases will sometimes do so, but it is risky to depend on it. A marten is fortunately almost certain to come back, though it may keep one waiting many anxious hours. Scores of times I have had mine go off on their own, but only one has finally walked out on me in this way, though seven or eight others have got out accidentally and gone wild. One of these is known to have lived wild for two years and another for at least three.

One of the first climbing tricks I taught my martens was to go up a long pole which I had baited with food at the top. I now make it more interesting by using a fresh-cut 30 foot larch, baiting the topmost twig which bends alarmingly when the animal approaches the food. Another stunt is to sweep the martinet over a line of 15-foot posts set about a yard apart, so that the martens will race along the tops of them after it. Various tight-rope turns add variety to this performance.

A marten's hearing is acute, so I attached a hawk-bell to the martinet to help them to locate the reward. When I felt I had reasonable control over them I began to take them to an adjoining wood. On a cord from my neck I hung a container with food, leaving both hands free to manipulate the martinet, the handle of which I had greatly lengthened with two joined bamboo poles. By raising this I encouraged the martens to climb and jump from tree to tree. Now the real fun began. There is something squirrel-like in the way they clasp a tree trunk with side-stretched limbs and jerk their way up or down, but the bark of some trees – beech, for example – may be too smooth for them to climb the trunks: their claws cannot grip it. They are expert in assessing instantly whether a particular route from one tree to another is negotiable and in spotting an alternative, which may mean going back to the trunk and out on another branch. A troupe racing wildly through a wood, all eager for the reward in the martinet, is a remarkable sight. After this strenuous and exciting exercise the martens usually go back readily to their pens.

Some years ago I found an interesting way of hunting with a marten. Blondin, then my favourite and a talented tree climber, was exercised regularly in the wood and on one occasion discovered a rabbit in some bushes. He sprang on it and killed it. This encouraged me to take him out hunting. The method was to get him to enter likely bushes by throwing in a scrap of food. Sometimes he would scent or see a rabbit and try to capture it by a sudden rush. When one broke cover with Blondin in full pursuit I had a revelation. I had always thought that martens were built for endurance rather than speed, but the rabbit, racing away from cover with a five-yard start, was only a couple of yards ahead when it had travelled about twenty yards, though after that it began to pull away. I had grossly underestimated the marten's acceleration.

Blondin generally caught his rabbits before they had time to get going. Occasionally he got one after a chase of up to a hundred yards, usually when it took refuge in other bushes. I saw no evidence of the rabbits being inhibited by fear: they seemed to move as quickly as if chased by a dog, perhaps because the marten did not follow them under-ground and bolt them from their burrows. I did not encourage Blondin to go to ground because I should have been able to recover few, if any, of the rabbits he killed. In proportion to its size a full-grown rabbit is one of the strongest of prey, and I was astonished that a marten could hold on to one and kill it: Blondin's total bag in the year before myxomatosis reached us was twenty-eight. He also killed a good-sized rat, a mole, a dormouse and, unfortunately, two or three birds in thick cover. In addition he caught field mice, which he hunted with stiff-legged jumps, as other animals do.

When I went hunting with Blondin I did not take the martinet but a walking-stick with a hawk bell attached to the handle. This helped him to find me in thick cover, though he would also come to my whistle. I think he chiefly relied on sight and scent to keep in touch with me. I used the stick also to pry into dense bushes and recover rabbits from thick brambles; Blondin always left them when they were dead. I am still puzzled by the way Blondin followed me close at heel. After dashing off in pursuit of a rabbit he would waste little time in returning if the quarry eluded him. We expect a dog to follow its master, but a marten is surely a lone hunter; why should it deliberately accompany a human being? I suspect that the reason is fundamentally the urge for food – the reason that prompts a falcon to wait on – whereas the dog's attachment to its master is largely the pack animal's craving for company.

I have had exceptional opportunities to observe what my martens will eat. I have known them catch frogs. Most ranch-bred martens will refuse slugs, but I had one which would drag them about under his front feet to de-slime them before eating them. All are fond of beetles and moths, and they will pick blackberries and rowan berries. So their diet can be very varied.

Not many generations ago martens were widespread in the British Isles. Now they have been banished from most of the country, surviving most successfully in the north of Scotland. They also exist as rarities in Wales, Ireland and the Lake District. The species cannot stand up to intensive persecution because its reproduction rate is low. Martens do not reach breeding age until they are two years old, and even then they produce only one litter, averaging three cubs, a year. They are not likely to become numerous because only a limited population is found even in virgin forests where they have never been hunted. If a few were present in our woodlands they would help to check the grey squirrel.

Seven Lame Badgers   *by Janet Orchard*

ONCE when my brother and I were badger watching in late August we saw six good-sized cubs leave the set, followed by a curious little creature not much bigger than a hedgehog. This was the dilling of the litter – small and stunted but very pert. After playing round the set on a heap of sand the cubs filed down a narrow path quite close to us, Dilly in the rear. They disappeared over a small ditch and up a bank on the far side into a thick clump of rhododendrons. There we heard much rustling of leaves and occasional growls and snufflings. When the troop reappeared about twenty minutes later, it was almost too dark to see. They filed past within a few feet of us, and to our amazement all seemed to be lame. We were mystified by this and determined to discover the cause.

Every evening for nearly a week we went to the same place, and exactly the same thing happened: the cubs all went out sound and came home lame. At last we were able to watch the return journey by the light of a good moon and saw each cub hobbling home on three legs; with the fourth it clasped to its chest a pawful of leaves, evidently stripped from the rhododendrons on the far bank. Dilly came last again and missed his footing as he crossed the ditch, dropping his leaves in mid-stream. His look of dismay as he set to work retrieving them was a wonderful sight. As soon as he picked up one he dropped another, but after exactly ten minutes of determined effort (timed by my brother's wrist-watch) Dilly limped home triumphantly clasping his small bunch of leaves.

Meanwhile the mother, with much snuffling and grunting, had raked the bedding clear of the set and sorted out all the dirt, which she carefully buried in the sand. She took the cleaned bedding and the fresh leaves brought by the cubs into the set and finally disappeared backwards, raking in Dilly's load as she went. After listening to the thuds and grunts of the underground bed-making, we decided to go home too, having solved a great mystery, though we still do not know if what we saw is common practice among badgers or peculiar to this one family.

Calling the Wild

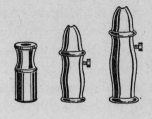

by Henry Tegner

SURPRISINGLY little is known in Britain about the art of calling wild animals, though this must be one of man's oldest skills. It is still practised in Africa, India and elsewhere by hunters who try to attract birds and beasts, in much the same way as primitive man must have done, for food. In Southern Rhodesia I had a Makaraki tracker who could call antelope with a high-pitched *pee-yew* which resembled the call made by German *jäger* to attract roebucks.

For more than twenty years I have specialized in trying to call roe-deer, not only with the object of shooting bucks but also with a view to closer study. I am still far from expert, but I have had some exciting moments. I recall an old buck that I hunted for several years in Dorset, in the oak woods round Milton Abbas. One August, during the time of the rut, I decided to try to lure him to me with a call. Knowing well the open glade he frequented in the early dawn and at dusk, I settled myself at the foot of a big oak one evening and started piping. If it was not he who came within 10 feet of where I sat, some other roebuck was tracking round out of sight behind the tree; but in the end he must have decided that I was up to no good, for with a succession of deep angry barks he galloped off into the woods. One August, when the rut of the roe was late in Northumberland, I went into a little wood where I knew there was a buck, sat motionless on a shooting-stick and did my calling. A fox cub came within 5 feet of me. When it saw me it crinkled its nose – I have seldom seen a more certain look of disgust – turned and trotted away. I moved a little deeper into the wood and started to call again. This time a red roebuck came rushing through the bracken. Like Charles St John I let him go, though I had my rifle with me; he made such a handsome figure.

While originally men probably used their own voices to mimic wild creatures, many devices have since been made for the purpose, most of them resembling flutes or trumpets. The roe-deer call common on the Continent is in the form of a small whistle or flute; I have a set of three, which are intended to represent the call of the fawn for its mother, that of the doe for her mate, and the fighting grunt of the rutting buck. I have not been particularly successful with the last, but with the others I have had some excellent results. North American Indians used to imitate moose with a bugle made of birch bark, now largely superseded by metal and plastic instruments. Some of the gadgets designed by man to deceive animals are extremely quaint. In a German sports shop I saw a great variety, including one that looked like an ancient bulb motor-horn; but instead of giving a deep road-clearing note it produced a trifling *peep-peep*, supposed to resemble the call of a love-lorn doe.

Among artists at luring birds and beasts one of the greatest I have met was a Belgian keeper in the Ardennes, Jules Warland, who used to carry a leather bag full of calls. One that imitated a stricken hare was most life-like and, I believe, very effective for enticing foxes. He also had a shrieking call to resemble the cry of a love-lorn vixen. An English expert, Arthur White, who was a keeper on the Milton Abbey estates near Blandford when I knew him, never used manufactured calls. He could summon a dog fox by a vocal imitation of an in-season vixen, though I never understood how the strange noise, like Highland pipes in distress, could deceive the fox. Arthur White also lured weasels and stoats with a high-pitched squeak made by sucking the back of his hand. This cry, in imitation of the shriek of a rodent in pain or terror, is not always easily heard by the human ear.

To become a successful caller requires patience and much practice. It appears to be essential to have a good ear for the finer nuances of animal voices; it is useless, for example, to bellow in imitation of a roaring stag without having previously listened attentively. On the other hand many animals are possessed of a strong curiosity which, I am convinced, sometimes makes them respond to a call having no resemblance to any they know.

LINED UP AT THE DOOR by Francis Dickie

During their first year in a fir forest in British Columbia, with food, kindness and patience, Mr Kym and his wife made friends with several families of wild racoons. They began with four; now as many as a dozen may visit them, arriving behind a leader who rattles on the back-door knob; the troupe then line up and wait to be invited in. After hearing names given to them repeated for a month, one family would take food in turn, advancing as their names were called.

The coon ranges across North America from the Atlantic to the Pacific. In intelligence it ranks close to the elephant, as has been shown by tests at the Bronx Zoo, New York. Coons escaped quickly from puzzle boxes which had completely baffled dogs and cats. In one test they had to press two pedals, pull a string, lift a latch, slide a bolt and undo a hook, yet several required less than a minute to gain freedom or food.

NINE POINTS OF THE LAW by Ida Watson

One evening we noticed a beautifully rounded hole in the flower border under our Devon bank. Next morning it was carefully filled in with leaves, but another hole had been freshly dug near by and left open with a mound of earth in front of it, down which were sharp claw marks. Towards dusk, a large rat ran along the front of the border and peered into the hole. Instantly the air was filled with snarling sounds and something white and furry, with snapping teeth, appeared in the entrance. The rat darted back, waited a minute and then approached again more cautiously. We remembered that for three evenings we had seen two rats go in and out of the border with leaves and grass, evidently making a nest. At the second approach a white paw shot out viciously and clawed the cheek of the rat, which squealed. Evidently the weasel had young ones to protect, for it struck repeatedly like lightning, growling and snarling all the time, but never left the hole. The rat dashed backwards and forwards, squealing continuously and kicking grit and soil over the weasel. Both were so absorbed that they did not notice us watching them. At last the rat turned round, shot out its back legs and sent shower after shower of sand, leaves, twigs and earth over the hole until this was completely covered. Then it cautiously approached and listened, before running slowly away battered and crestfallen, both cheeks scratched and bleeding. The weasel and its family remained in possession, and the rat colony in the garden moved to fresh quarters.

ned up at the door – wild coons waiting to be invited in

badger who has forgotten
cut his nails

Collecting Foxes

by Gay A. Sagar

NEARLY twenty years ago I was telling a farmer friend how much I would like to have a fox cub as a pet, and there and then he produced one – not out of a hat but from a sack. Ever since, fox cubs have been brought to me in sacks, boxes and other containers.

There was Barny, who had been found apparently abandoned at the age of about two months. I decided that he would have to accompany me whenever I went and so be accustomed to seeing a lot of people from the start. Every day he accompanied me to the office and curled up on a shelf by my desk, sleeping nearly all the time. Fortunately the factory was in the country, so I could take him for a lunch-time walk on his lead. If I went to see a film he had to come too. Cinema managers are not madly keen to have livestock on their premises; but how were they to know, when I walked in with a fox fur over my arm, that the bright eyes and quivering nose of Barny were tucked inside my coat? And if two people bought three tubs of ice-cream, in the dark no one could see a greedy fox cub licking his tub with relish. Barny seemed a success at first, but for one reason and another I had to leave him a good deal on his own and he became so timid with everyone else that it made me miserable. At last I let him go, and although I called him every evening for a time I did not see him again. If only, I sighed, one could have a cub that was free.

Not long afterwards I met a woman who was a whipper-in to a pack of foxhounds. She told me that she had had a very young cub and brought him up in her house with the hunt terriers. He went to live in the field next to the house when he was older, and stayed for about three years. I asked whether she had ever worried about the hounds hunting him. She told me how, when she was watching one side of a covert near home and listening to hounds working on the other, the fox Charlie bounded out very pleased to see her. Quietly she ordered him to go home, and he disappeared again into the undergrowth. Later a check on the time of his arrival at the kennels showed that he must have returned immediately after she had spoken to him.

This story stirred in me a longing to have a free fox and the following year, when the R.S.P.C.A. inspector rang me up late one evening to say that he had another cub, this time injured, I agreed at once to have him. A poor weak creature, he had been rescued from a trap. How long he had been without food I have no idea, but for several days we had to feed him with milk from a spoon. At first we added a few drops of whisky, from which he got his name. Whisky was quite the most lovable cub I had ever had. Although, from the beginning, when I picked him up he would cough at me in the peculiar way of a fox – rather like a cat spitting – as soon as I began to bathe his injured leg he would lick my hand and sit quite still. There were times when I must have hurt him a great deal, but he never attempted to draw his leg away. I thought of the reactions of most dogs and cats to any kind of treatment and felt that the old story of removing the thorn from the lion's foot might well be true. I had Whisky for about three months. He gradually grew stronger and his leg healed, but he also was too old to tame; as he began to feel better he started to scratch at the wall to get out. Regretfully I released him one night, leaving his basket in a quiet spot with food beside it. I was overjoyed when he obviously returned at night to eat; but I did not see him again, and after a week the food remained untouched.

After this last disappointment I decided that I would never achieve my ambition of having a fox cub as a pet and at the same time quite free. While I was ruminating about such things a large van stopped in the drive and a man got out. As he came up to me carrying a cardboard box, he began, 'I've got a——' 'Oh, no,' I interrupted, 'not a fox cub'. He looked startled: 'Why yes, I found it on the road; its leg is a bit hurt.' That is how I came to have Foxy, who had no other name because I was so sure she would not be with us long. She was a weedy-looking object the size of a large kitten – about seven weeks old, I guessed. As she was still too young to care for herself, we decided that we would have to keep her for a while. She soon became quite tame with the children and me, but like the others she remained very afraid of everyone she did not know. I took her about with me for a week or two, but it is difficult to carry a fox cub without being continually stopped by people who want to look at it; so I gave up trying to introduce her to the world at large.

I had not before realized how much foxes love sweet things. Foxy would go crazy for bread and syrup or sweet milky coffee – in fact, anything really sugary. She lived happily with us for a month or so, becoming very attached to our Alsatian bitch Belga, with whom she played every evening. Belga was thirteen and a great character; she was often likened to Nana in *Peter Pan*. One of her greatest virtues was her kindly acceptance of any animal we happened to adopt. At first Foxy was very hostile to her, but her unruffled calm, even when attacked by this wretched little cub, made Foxy realize that here was a friend.

In spite of all we did to make Foxy happy, she began to show all the signs of wanting to be free. After about six weeks I could bear it no longer, but this time I made some preparations before releasing her. I started to take her for walks on a collar and lead in the garden down to an old rabbit-hole where a dachshund had once followed a rabbit and had to be dug out. It made an ideal earth, as it was well screened with bushes. After showing Foxy the way to it from all directions, one evening about a week later I set her free. She rushed round and round with the greatest joy but, to our amazement, did not run away. She played for a full two hours that evening, never still for a minute. When I retired to bed about midnight, I wondered if I would see her again.

In the morning I went to the entrance of her new home and called. At first there was no movement, but in a minute she popped out of the hole. As she stood and looked at me, gradually her ears went back and she began to wag her tail, very slowly at first. Then, as if she had suddenly decided that it really was me, she bounded forward and jumped up like a puppy, tail wagging furiously. We were very excited; at last a fox was staying with us of its own accord. For several nights I left open the door of the place where she had been sleeping, until I knew that she was perfectly content in her new home. Obviously she called in, for her new collar and lead vanished unaccountably. Other things, too, disappeared mysteriously, and if anything was missing we looked for it at the entrance of her earth; bathing-trunks, towels, etc., have all been found there.

We did not see much of Foxy during the day, though she came out whenever she was called, so long as no strangers were about. Belga took to calling her, going to the hole, sticking her head down and whining until Foxy appeared. This odd pair were really fond of one another. In the evenings the cub was about the garden all the time and played with Belga as long as the dog would stay out with her, being especially fond of jumping on Belga's back and lying there until she was shaken off. When I saw how much energy Foxy used running round and wrestling with Belga, I realized how impossible it was to keep an animal so full of vitality contented in captivity. Belga unfortunately died in September, and a few weeks later I bought an Alsatian puppy, which I introduced to Foxy. They soon made friends and began to romp about the garden; and they continued to play every evening when Foxy called.

One evening in June, when she had been with us for more than a year, Foxy came and took away a lot of food, returning several times for more. I was sure she had cubs not far away and was excited at the prospect of her bringing them with her when they were old enough. The following evening I sat in the garden until midnight and was puzzled that she did not appear. When I made inquiries next day I learnt that a vixen had been trapped not far away. The garden seemed empty in the evenings without the mischievous brown shadow that was Foxy. For days I searched the fields, calling her, but I never saw her again.

NOSE BETWEEN PAWS

I spent my early days in the Vale of Belvoir with Long Clawson Thorns only 50 yards from our door. One day as I sat on a fence beside a brook by the covert I heard the faint echo of a hunting horn and a few minutes later saw a fox padding leisurely towards me. He ran calmly down the bank into the stream and along it a little way, then climbed into the fork of a hollow willow and lay 'nose in between paws', like John Masefield's Reynard, not 12 yards from me. When the hounds reached the spot they checked, and in the end the huntsman called them off. Presently the fox rose, stretched himself, came down again into the water and passed close to me.

C. W. R. Cragg, Leicestershire

Wild Deer in Britain

by Gerald Johnstone

AT least six species of deer live wild in Britain, some of them in considerable numbers; but few people seem to know how to distinguish them, or where they may be seen. The largest is the red deer, and no one obtaining a clear view of an adult could well mistake it, if only because it is a foot taller than any other species at present found wild here, the stag averaging 4 feet in height and the hind only a fraction less. In certain areas – Lundy Island and Aberdeenshire among them – our native race has interbred with the wapiti, the red deer of North America and parts of Asia, which may stand as much as 5 feet 4 inches high. The British race is dark reddish brown, though some individuals are sandy coloured, and there would be a tendency to yellowish grey in those with wapiti blood. The calf is born spotted and retains its baby coat for about four months. Red deer are more widely distributed, at all events as regular 'travellers', than is generally realized. I have notes of them from all southern counties except Kent, and from the west Midlands, East Anglia and the North, as well as Scotland.

Still more common is the fallow deer, which one may expect to find in any heavily wooded and reasonably wild country. The vast majority are the descendants of deer which have escaped from parks in the last twenty to thirty years, but unenclosed herds have always existed in the New Forest, Epping Forest and possibly other areas. The buck stands about 3 feet high, and the doe is rather smaller.

The typical fallow deer is light brown in colour, the upper parts of the back and flanks being fairly profusely spotted with white in the summer months; but in almost every herd one sees a number of very dark animals (almost black in some cases), and competent observers say that these do not interbreed with the lighter ones, although they mingle with

them both in a wild state and in semi-captivity in parks. White animals
are rare among red deer, but are common among fallow deer, few herds
being without their share. Whether light, dark or white, the buck is
distinguished from all other British species by his palmated antlers; at
some distance from the head they broaden out into flattish areas of horn,
which may be likened very roughly to the palm of a hand; and round the
edges there are relatively short promontories suggestive of fingers.

This antler formation is the surest way of telling a fallow buck in
summer pelage from the male of an Indian species, the chital or axis
deer (*Axis axis*), occasional specimens of which have been seen in the
counties just north, and also apparently south, of the Thames. This
animal stands about the same height as the fallow, and is a member of
the sambur family; it is very heavily spotted with white at all seasons,
the area of the coat thus covered extending well up the neck and almost
under the belly – another point of distinction. The antlers of the buck
ascend more or less straight up from the head instead of sweeping out
in the glorious curve which adds so much to the majesty of the red stag,
and the formation is extremely simple, consisting of a brow antler and
beam with a single inner tine.

Another deer of about the same height which has been reported from
the mosses on the Scottish Border is the American black-tailed deer
(*Mazama columbiana*). This animal is a sandy brown in colour, tending
towards grey in its winter coat, and has a simple formation of antlers of
the normal forked type. It is said to be the most prodigious jumper of
the whole deer family.

Next in size comes the sika deer (*Sika nippon*), originally introduced from both Japan and the mainland opposite, but usually loosely
called the Japanese deer. This animal stands about 2 feet 8 inches high,
and the buck has forked antlers. The Japanese race is of a warm brown
colour with a pronounced white rump and with the upper parts of the
pelage spotted with white in the summer. Those from the mainland
(Manchuria and Korea) are much darker, with pale lemonish yellow
spots and buffish rumps. Unlike the two races of fallow deer, the sikas
appear to interbreed freely, so that where both types occur, as they do
over much of the south of England and the Midlands, the characteristics

described above may become confused. The size of the animals will, however, remain constant and should be a safe guide to identification.

The roe-deer is to my mind the most attractive of all our native wild species. Standing just over 2 feet in height and of a very compact build, the British race of roe is a dark reddish brown in colour. The buck carries short spiky horns (I cannot bring myself to call them antlers) which run to as many as six tiny points. A denizen of thick woods, this species is to be found in suitable localities over the whole of the mainland of Scotland and in the north of England down at least to a line drawn from Morecambe Bay to the mouth of the Tees. It has been reintroduced into Dorset and East Anglia, and from both those places has spread out wonderfully.

At some period in the last twenty or thirty years the Siberian roe (*Capreolus pygargus*) escaped from captivity in Bedfordshire and it has acclimatized itself in the woods of that county, Buckinghamshire and Northamptonshire. Isolated individuals have pushed along the Chilterns and crossed the Thames. It is, therefore, at least possible that it may be encountered anywhere within a seventy-mile radius of Ampthill Forest, where it was first reported in a wild state. It is taller and paler than our native roe (nearly as tall as a sika deer), has correspondingly longer horns, and is fawn in colour.

Two other small Asiatic deer are to be found wild in England; one certainly, and the other presumably, originated in Bedfordshire. These are the Chinese water deer (*Hydropotes inermis*) and the muntjac, or barking deer, of which two races, the typical Indian *Muntiacus muntjak* and the smaller Chinese *Muntiacus reevesi*, have escaped. The water deer is a long, low animal of distinctly sheep-like build. Its average height is said to be about 1 foot 8 inches and its colour is a bright brown. The buck is hornless, but is armed with tusks. I have never seen this deer in rapid motion, but understand that it proceeds with a series of clumsy bounds and tires rapidly. It has been reported from most of the counties bordering on Bedfordshire and Hampshire.

The Indian muntjac was turned down in the coverts at Woburn towards the end of the last century, and was stated by Lyddekker, in

A roe deer and her yearling buck resting in the sun in Westmorland, their colour blending with the background

Alarmed, they turn to flee, no longer inconspicuous because their white
tail-patches betray them

Even in summer, when food is plentiful, this old red deer
came to a cottage in the Cairngorms for titbits

his book *Deer of All Lands,* to have been quite common there, though rarely seen, by the beginning of the present century. Since the creation of the Whipsnade deer parks, specimens of the Chinese race also have escaped, and interbreeding must have taken place because at least one shot deer has been pronounced by experts to be a hybrid. Having a good start over the other species which originated in the same localities, the barking deer have got a good way farther off also. They have been reported from the northern outskirts of the New Forest and from the vicinity of Matlock in Derbyshire, both more than a hundred miles from Woburn. If they have spread out evenly in all directions, they must be pretty widely distributed.

The Indian race, at 1 foot 9 inches, is a little taller than the water deer, but the Chinese barking deer is very small, seldom rising above 1 foot 2 inches. Its colour is reddish brown, whereas the Indian is a dark chocolate shade, but manifestly where both races occur animals will be seen of varying shades and of heights ranging between the maximum and minimum set out above. The species as a whole is unique. The bucks, in addition to their small size, can be recognized by their short upright horns, the bone structure of which continues down the face, producing a decidedly ugly effect and giving rise to the subsidiary name of ribbed deer. The front legs are short, and although this animal is more compact and less clumsily built than the water deer, I should say that its powers of sustaining a rapid pace were if anything less. The doe is a hornless edition of her ugly husband.

I ought perhaps to add that the last three species are not herd deer, but live either in pairs, or at most in small family parties of four or five. This fact, together with their relatively small size, may cause them to be overlooked, even in districts where they are not uncommon.

Wild Deer

With laurel ears leaf-pricked into the wind
Here comes a shy and solitary hind.
And all the forest sighs; the small wind dies;
And every timid creature shrinks behind
A guardian tree to find a cloak of shade.

Her nostrils flare, for danger scents the air
And Fear runs trembling through the patterned glade.
For this were wild deer made –
To walk on twigs of fear when man comes near?

Hesitant deer now tense with pent-up breath,
Now snuffing the mild wood striped with tiger shade,
Rigid a moment in the poise of death,
Then loosed in flight that makes the earth afraid.

The loyal wind has turned about and given
The hind a shout of friendship – watch her go
Quiet and sure as though she stepped on snow;
And the herd is grazing down green slopes of heaven.

Phoebe Hesketh

Otters at Close Quarters

by H. S. Joyce

A LIFE-LONG passion for fishing has given me many opportunities for observing otters. As a schoolboy I spent almost every day of my holidays, usually alone, on a quiet and secluded river regularly inhabited by them. In later years, when fishing for trout by day in some of the remoter rivers of the west of England, and for sea-trout at night, I frequently had intimate views of them. I soon learnt that fish, including eels, are by no means their sole diet. Opportunity mainly determines the type of food they take; it may be almost any kind of flesh. In my experience they have often caught pike, usually a fish weighing 2–3 lb., from which they have eaten a good chunk from the shoulder; so also chub and roach. Moorhens have been frequent victims, and frogs when they came to water in spring. Occasionally an otter would take up temporary residence in a rabbit burrow and kill and eat the occupants, which it seemed always to take to a sort of dining-table among the rushes beside the river; there the flesh was eaten and the skin turned inside out.

Wild duck have fallen victims at times, and I once saw an otter seize a mallard that had just alighted on the water, and climb out on the opposite bank with the bird in its mouth. I have also known them to kill and carry off domestic ducks. A few years ago some were taken from a farm in our neighbourhood and a fox was suspected. Hearing a great commotion one day by the stream, the farmer rushed with his gun to the spot and saw three otters, one with a duck in its mouth. He shot two and lost no more birds. In very hard weather otters will sometimes kills lambs, footprints proving them and not a fox to be the culprits; but this cannot be regarded as a regular or even a common habit.

Otters rarely seem to kill for the sake of killing. As with nearly all beasts of prey, however, a blood-lust will seize them if they find themselves surrounded by a host of creatures unable to escape them, such as young trout in a hatchery. In a natural state they rarely kill more than they require at the moment, though one may sometimes take a larger fish than it can eat at a meal. I have seen several salmon that have been killed by otters, and every one has been dragged out of the water, usually on to a rock in midstream where, as with pike, a meal was taken from the shoulder and the rest left to the rats. I think most anglers will agree that when an otter enters a sea-trout pool it is useless to continue fishing. But I have known brown trout to feed freely within a quarter of an hour after an otter had hunted the rock-edges in which they sheltered.

Though otters usually hunt by night, they will sometimes feed in daylight. On very quiet rivers I have frequently seen them hunting during the day. At Dulverton one used to cross the river as soon as it heard any refuse thrown into the water and would feed in full view of the road on the rabbit paunches thrown out by the cottagers.

The Indian trappers of North America are said to know the overland routes of otters and to trap them there, often at considerable distances from rivers. These routes seem to be recognized by the otters from generation to generation, though they may remain unused for long periods. There is evidence of similar traditional overland routes in this country, and I have known several instances of otters being seen on such supposed trails, which usually cross a watershed between two streams. I have myself been called on by the police to remove an otter from a coal-shed in the built-up area of a large town which was on a direct route between two streams, though at a considerable distance from both. I believe that some otters live almost always by the sea. In certain quiet rocky coves on the coasts of Devon and Cornwall you may see the evidences of them at almost any time of the year, and the animals themselves if you have the patience to lie hidden and wait.

I have heard of only one unprovoked attack on a human being by an otter and am inclined to think that this may have been because the person was in a position suggesting to the animal that he intended to prevent it entering its holt, which probably contained cubs. I have never even thought of the possibility of being attacked, though many times I have been within a few feet of an otter. One placed its paws on the toe of my boot as I stood close to the edge of the water, and we looked at each other for a second or two; then it quietly sank and continued upstream.

OTTERS AND CUBS

No one who has heard the otter's distinctive whistle – a sound which many human ears fail to register – is likely to forget it. When it came to me on the wind as I walked the bank of a Highland stream I sank into a clump of ferns and waited. It was quite close when I next heard it, and a long shadowy form was moving upstream leaving a double chain of bubbles. Two more lines of bubbles marked the course of cubs. Then the deep pool near by rippled and danced as all three dived and chased each other from bank to bank. Now and again a shining body would leap into the air, or one of the cubs would abandon itself to the rushing water and float away with just the tip of its rudder-like tail showing, only to turn and dart back again as swiftly as if it were swimming with the strong current instead of against it. After some ten minutes' play the mother gave the cubs a few lessons. She showed them how to take a trout from below, then reared herself up to watch their efforts. Again and again she dived and bobbed up, chasing them if they lost interest and started to play. Presently she moved across stream and climbed the opposite bank. The cubs followed and waited expectantly, while their mother, with the curious loping gallop of the otter, made her way to the roots of an old tree by the water's edge. Then like a flash she was in the stream. After a long submersion she came up with a sizeable fish in her jaws, and the cubs raced along the bank to meet her. They tore and bit at the fish while she held it, till only the head was left. Then the mother dived into the water, calling the cubs to follow. At first I thought she had sensed my presence, but all three swam quietly past my hiding-place without a glance. *Alan Duncan*

Mongoose versus Cobra

by D. B. J. McTurk

IN the hills of Holkar there was an accredited snake expert, an old Dutch planter, who had been amusing us with tales of his experiences. We had, of course, asked him if he had seen a mongoose in action, but this he denied. Soon I received a message: he had a cobra, newly caught; a mongoose had easily been procured: he arranged a pit; would I come?

Our friend had done his job thoroughly. The pit was of sand and about twenty feet across, so placed in a hollow in the ground that we stood about 6 feet above it. Immediately on our arrival he introduced the snake, a big one, perhaps 4 feet long, and it slithered uneasily away from its basket and lay, half coiled, an evil, venomous creature. When the mongoose was placed on the opposite side, it appeared at once indifferent to its circumstances – sat down, scratched and shook itself.

The snake had reacted immediately by raising itself on its coils, its hood slowly extending. It must have made some sound, for the non-chalance of its antagonist vanished instantly. The mongoose's fur began to bristle, its tail to enlarge. With a sort of stiffened walk, menacing and determined, it approached the cobra. It stopped a yard short, sat up on its haunches, slightly swaying, its eyes now ruby-red.

It was the snake that moved first, but so quickly that we could tell that it had struck only by the stirring of the sand; it was back in its position, alert and vigilant, before we had seen its movement. Again it struck, and this time we were better prepared; even so, true observation was almost impossible. We could judge, however, by the rising dust and the distinct thud that the blow was heavy – far heavier than one would have expected. The result was the same: still each was poised, deadly; still the same watchful silence.

It took us some time to appreciate their tactics and limitations. The snake, its coils to the rear of its neck, and head high above its antagonist, could strike only forwards in a small arc and downwards. The mongoose appeared unwilling to shift the position of its hind legs and merely swayed sideways as the snake struck, relying on the speed and control of its actions, and probably also on the thickness of its fur, to avoid the destruction which one direct blow would have meant. So far it had shown no inclination to close to the attack.

At the end of ten minutes the first round was over. The cobra, exhausted by its own powerful blows, lay stretched on the ground at full length, the tight coils loosened. Surely now would come the *coup de grâce*! But again we were to be surprised. Infinitely wary, the mongoose dropped to its forefeet and moved in a wide circle to approach from behind. Lightly and swiftly it pounced on the tip of the snake's tail and away again: once more, and the coils began slowly to tighten, the hooded head to rise. The snake had revived, and the battle began once more.

The result was now no longer in doubt. The blows of the cobra, half stunned, were slower, its recovery more laboured. The mongoose, never for a moment slackening its attention, appeared fresh and confident. Exactly ten more minutes sufficed. The snake's energy was now completely spent, and it failed a second time to rise. As cautious as before, the mongoose made the same approach. There was no response, either to this or to other verifying attacks. Even so the matter must evidently be considered; with head on one side, the glow receding from its eyes, it stood for fully two minutes before severing the senseless neck.

CAT'S COURAGE

In Nyasaland a friend of mine was sitting in her drawing-room on a warm evening with the french windows wide open and only a black cat and her kittens for company. All was quiet when a leopardess walked in from the veranda. Instantly the cat flew at the intruder and clung to its face, biting and clawing. The leopardess bolted outside, and there was a tremendous noise of veranda furniture being knocked about. My friend was still too taken aback even to get up when the noise ceased and the cat went quietly to her kittens.

Isabel Talbot, Nyasaland

TOADS' DEFENCES

by Leonard G. Appleby

The acid fluid that exudes from the numerous glands and warts on the backs of toads does not deter some grass-snakes from eating toads, though the majority will not touch them. I myself have witnessed a grass-snake swallowing a toad and watched the bulge in its stomach become slowly smaller as the toad was digested with no outward sign of ill effects for the snake. The unfortunate toad may then appear to have no means of defence except that of lying doggo; but I have watched one defend itself by another method.

The toad shared a small enclosure in my garden with a grass-snake, which showed no interest in it at first, having recently eaten a frog. Once the frog had been digested, however, the snake awoke from its lethargy and began to watch the toad's slow peregrinations about the enclosure in search of a way of escape. Slowly the snake's head turned, as it followed the toad with its stony gaze. Its long, black, divided tongue came out and wavered slowly up and down, and then it slid forward over the moss-covered floor with effortless grace. When the toad became aware of the snake's approach, it halted, blinked one bulging eye and gave a gulp. The snake came on relentlessly, its cold stare fixed on the toad, which shuffled its feet uncomfortably, blinked again and then froze into stillness; the only sign of life was the pulsing of its throat. The snake also stopped, stared hard at the toad, its tongue moving slowly in and out, and then went forward again over the green moss. The toad did not move until the snake's flickering tongue tickled its warty back, when it fidgeted uncontrollably, gulped even harder and bent its snout nearer the ground. Then the snake began to glide over the toad's back as though it was just a stone; whereupon the toad closed its eyes and reared up on all fours with such suddenness that the snake was thrown almost a foot away. It hissed angrily, as it rolled over on to its belly, but made no attempt to attack the toad, which had again frozen into immobility.

Twice that day I saw the same thing happen and was reminded of the behaviour of a toad that I found in the garden one summer evening. It, too, had reared up on its four legs when I touched its back, and remained shakily in that position for some seconds.

BEDTIME SNACK?

I have a springer spaniel who likes to collect snails during his last walk after supper. He generally finds two or three, but in wet weather has disgorged as many as seven on returning to his basket.

H. C. Milne, Hants

Common toads mating in a pool near the Potteries. Swimming under water, the male remains firmly attached to the back of the larger female before and during egg-laying

BATTLE ROYAL

by Anne Quekett

As I sat on a rocky platform on the eastern side of Rathlin Island, some four miles off the north Antrim coast, I was startled to hear heavy breathing almost at my feet and saw that a big grey bull seal had come close inshore to inspect me. After some minutes he disappeared and I was looking for his partner, as seals are not often seen singly, when there was a sudden turmoil just off the rocks. The bull rose grunting and wheezing in his effort to maintain his grip on a giant conger-eel, which he held near the tail. The giant length of the eel's body arched high out of the water and then flattened along the surface. While the seal tried to take a surer grip near the head, the conger reared its gleaming coils up and above the seal's head, striking at the jaws and finally twisting in a stranglehold about the thick bull-neck. Time after time the pair submerged and rose struggling together, until the eel released its grip momentarily and was seized beneath the head and bitten deep in the belly, so that the water was crimson about them.

The seal now began to show signs of distress. He seemed to rest briefly, unable to do more than keep his hold on the eel, which was still fighting gamely, the slap of its tail sounding on the water and on its adversary's body. The end of the struggle was a breath-taking spectacle. The seal dipped his great head and, gripping the conger below the water with his flippers, raised himself slowly, drawing back his head; steadily he tore a long strip of living flesh from head to tail and devoured it. The sounds of tearing flesh and crunching jaws came sharply across to me on that still afternoon, until there remained only the tail and bared vertebræ, still lashing for release, though feebly now. Then these, too, were eaten to the last mouthful. Tired and replete, the seal heaved his great shining body on to the rock platform where, unconcerned at my presence, he lay basking in the last warmth of the sun. The whole struggle had occupied fully ten minutes.

THEN THERE WERE THREE

While I was fishing in an Irish lake a duck cruised by with four ducklings, one of which disappeared under water. I threw my spoon bait a few feet beyond the spot and almost immediately felt the pull of a fish. It was well hooked and soon landed: a pike close on 7 lb.

When I opened it I found the duckling inside. It was dead, of course, but bore no sign of teeth marks: the pike had apparently sucked it down in one gulp.

D. F. McCrea, Belfast

An eel nearly three feet in length on the first stage of its long journey from the Rhine to the Sargasso Sea

LYNCH LAW

On the veranda of my bungalow in the tropics I killed a cockroach and left it to see how soon it would be discovered by the ants that lived in the cracks between the floorboards. A solitary ant soon found the booty, failed to move it and dashed off for help. I removed the cockroach, but only just before a score of ants arrived with one an inch or two in the lead. It took the others straight to the spot where the prize had been; there it stopped, looked and then rushed round in circles as if in a panic. The others waited. When at last it returned they set on it with one accord and a few seconds later departed, leaving one dead ant.

R. T. Ruddick, Wilts

When I was a child in Lancashire the manager of a local bleachworks came to see my father one morning, much upset by an incident he had just witnessed. In a field next to the works he had noticed a rat stop to investigate something and then run away. Out of curiosity he had climbed the stone wall and found a dead hen, which he carried to the edge of the field. A few minutes later he saw about thirty rats making for the place where the hen had lain. When the rat leading the others reached the spot it gave a loud squeal, whereupon the rest immediately set on it and killed it.

Jessie B. Lush, Auckland, N.Z.

RATS ON THE MARCH

I was staying in County Tyrone in the early autumn and had gone for a long walk one afternoon with the dogs of the house: a collie, a cocker and a nondescript yard dog who was supposed to be a good ratter. Arriving rather breathless at the top of a steep hill, I decided to rest on a gate and saw the dogs racing up the hill behind me. They were no longer hunting in the hedges and every now and again paused to look back, seemingly frightened. As they came clustering round my feet I saw crossing the road at a point we had just passed an indescribable brown mass like clods of earth pouring from the ploughed field into the road.

Then I saw it was rats. There must have been thousands of them, fighting for space where the crowd was thickest. They kept to their mass formation, none attempting to come up the hill, and I stood watching until they were out of sight. Then, the dogs shaking with fear and I not feeling much braver, we hurried home. Later I learned that the nearby town had been having a rat week.

Decima Tate, Northumberland

A NEAR DISASTER

Our dogs had found a rat-hole under the gnarled roots of a giant Scots pine, which spread over the top of a bank and ran beneath a hawthorn. All day, at intervals, they had been on the bank trying to get at the nest. Then, towards sundown, I saw the mother rat come out with a baby in her mouth; evidently she had decided to find new quarters. Already a thin film of ice covered the water in the bird bath on the lawn, and the twigs of the hawthorn sparkled with hoar frost. The old rat stood still, her head raised anxiously, and sniffed the air; along the bank behind her ran six or seven more young rats. She raised herself on her hind legs and, still holding the baby, ran lightly along the larger branches of the hawthorn until she reached the middle of it, where it grew into a thicket. Then she turned and went down on the other side, carefully making her way between the branches, but the baby rat became caught between some thorny twigs. The mother stopped and tried to extricate it, pulling it gently this way and that, but without success. She stood on her hind legs and tried frantically with her front paws to get the little creature out. Suddenly there was a movement at the root of the pine and, like a streak of lightning another large rat dashed up the thorn-tree and on to the opposite branch. There followed one of the most remarkable displays of sagacity and determination I have ever seen, as the two old rats worked together, one carefully pushing and the other gently pulling, to free the baby. The frosty twigs shone and swayed as they slipped and turned, tugged and pushed, their bodies silhouetted against the crimson sunset. Finally the male rat bit the twigs and tore them away from the small body with his teeth, until at last it dangled free. Then he turned and ran away quickly, and the mother, again carrying the baby in her mouth, sped down the bush in the opposite direction.

Ida Watson, Devon

SPIRITED MOUSE

Friends of mine lean a post against the window-sill of their caravan on the outside so that their cats can enter or leave at night when the door is closed. One morning they saw in the van a mouse which must have entered by this ramp, for the mice which the cats bring in from the fields are invariably dead. In this mouse the cats took no interest, even when it helped itself to food from their dish under their very noses. It showed no inclination to leave by the open door or window, successfully eluding all human manœuvres to steer it out. A neighbour who chanced to call with two retrievers boasted that they would make short work of the unwanted guest, and one succeeded in cornering it, only to retire howling with a nipped nose. Neither could be persuaded to return to the attack. After three days the caravan-wife happened to catch the mouse sitting by the open door and swept it out. It did not return.

E. E. Gilbert, Denbighshire

The Little Crocus of Dawlish

by Alison Wilson

ONE of the choicer rarities among wild flowers in Britain is the Jersey crocus (*Romulea columnae*), which grows on the mainland only at Dawlish Warren, the sand-spit across the mouth of the River Exe. It is abundant there, but is likely to be seen only on a few warm, sunny, spring days round about noon. When open the flowers are about a centimetre across, the perianth leaves being a milky-blue, each with a central violet streak; the three anthers make a golden eye.

This Mediterranean plant was first noticed here in 1834, when the Warren was a sandy pasture. Ten years later, Amelia Griffiths, the Torquay botanist, had pleasure in sending her friend Sir William Hooker some of its tiny corms, which her daughter had gathered for him to grow at Kew. In her letter, which is preserved at the Herbarium, Mrs. Griffiths regretted that the plant's restricted habitat was to be invaded by the proposed new railway. Happily the crocus was not destroyed, and now grows extensively on the fairway of the golf-course.

DOG ROSE LEGEND

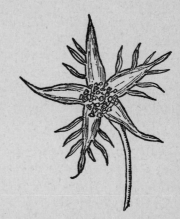

My grandfather, a landscape gardener, told me this old Cornish story about the five sepals of the dog rose. There were five brothers, each of whom had a beard. When two of them decided to shave theirs off, one of the others was in doubt what he should do, for while the two with beards urged him to keep his, the others begged him to shave it off. Whichever advice he followed would not meet with general approval. At last he had an idea to please them all: he shaved off one side only. If you examine a dog rose you will usually find that little points grow on both sides of two of the sepals; two are without points and the fifth has them on one side only. *Laura Foest*

114

The little Jersey crocus

The purple pasque flower,
a plant of the short turf of
chalk and limestone hills

The stinkhorn fungus   5 p.m.   8 p.m.

Next day   9 a.m.   11 a.m.

THE STINKHORN

by Douglas Swinscow

Despite its arresting appearance the stinkhorn fungus is more likely to be smelt than seen. Springing up from the leaf-mould in woods, it fills the air for some yards around with the penetrating sickly sweetish scent of rotting flesh. As the walker hurries past what he supposes to be the putrefying remains of some woodland animal, he may notice a cloud of flies which seems to confirm his suspicion; for, though repulsive to man, the stinkhorn depends on the attraction it exerts on flies for the efficient dispersal of its spores.

Mushrooms are traditionally supposed to spring up in a night, but I think the stinkhorn would beat them in the race fairly easily. It will expand from the 'egg' stage to its full height in six hours, or even less when conditions are favourable, the rate depending partly on the amount of free moisture in the soil. The specimen illustrated on the opposite page was growing in a wood of oak and hornbeam. The two top photographs were taken at 5 p.m. and 8 p.m., and those below at 9 a.m. and 11 a.m. the following day. By evening the fungus had collapsed and was prostrate on the ground.

Thick white threads–the vegetative condition of the fungus – traverse the top soil and leaf-mould on the woodland floor. Some time in the second half of summer a bud forms on one of the threads and swells to a whitish globe about the size of a hen's egg. At this stage the fungus, if cut open, is almost odourless; indeed it is said to be eaten in some parts of the world. At the centre is the solid white material that will soon form the stalk; the structure round it will produce spores and become the dark green cap; and outside that is a layer of jelly, the whole being contained in a firm skin. It is by expansion, not growth, that the fruiting body pushes up through its capsule, and as it does so the characteristic carrion smell is given off, attaining full strength when the stem is extended. Flies then come and eat the jelly, clearing away the spores with it. These are in due course excreted elsewhere and germinate better for having passed through the fly's digestive tract.

LARGEST PUFF-BALL?

A fine specimen of the giant puff-ball (*Lycoperdon giganteum*) was found at a spot where kennel bedding had been taken out into a meadow at Ascott-under-Wychwood; it was mistaken at first for a swan. It had a circumference of 72 inches, was 17 inches high and weighed 26 lb. 10 oz. This is apparently a British record, for the largest native specimen mentioned by Dr Ramsbottom in his book *Mushrooms and Toadstools* was 64 inches in circumference. The Ascott puff-ball may have contained more than 3120 billion spores.

J. M. Campbell, Oxon

Garden Fossils

by Duncan Forbes

FROM time to time in the newspapers there appears a snippet of news – a space-filler – telling us that somebody has found a fossil in his garden. It might read: 'Mr Smith, of Crowstead, unearthed a fossil sea-urchin when gardening. It is estimated by the curator of the local museum to be 100 million years old.' To readers unfamiliar with the nature of fossils the location may seem surprising and the age impressive: two of the essential ingredients of news. There is, however, nothing surprising in this information if the garden is over chalk, as fossil sea-urchins are common in the upper chalk and many other limestones. Those composed of flint are very hard-wearing, and when chalk is worn away by rivers or other agents they remain and are found with other flints in the resulting gravel.

Unless a fossil is found embedded in its native rock, it is seldom safe to assume that it belongs to the area. If Mr Smith had found his sea-urchin in the chalk under his soil, he could have been sure that it was in its original resting place 100 million years after it had sunk into the ooze on the bed of the warm sea which then covered this part of the world. But if, for instance, his garden is on a clay, the fossil must have been transported by a river or even the ice sheets of the Ice Age.

I know a garden in Kent with a sunken path cut in gault clay, in the sides of which are numerous fossil ammonites, or coiled shells. Another garden I visit, in Surrey, has boulders from the Atherfield beds just under the soil; this rock seldom comes to the surface north of the Isle of Wight and the boulders are full of beautiful fossil shells. Many Surrey and Sussex gardens have small cuttings in chalk, and I once surprised a friend by digging out a dozen or so species of fossil shells, sea-urchins and sponges from a 3-foot cutting. In another garden which I know, near Barton in Hampshire, the soil contains many shells which look as if they had been brought up from the beach by children, till one realizes that they belong to families now living off Australia, California and other warm places. It is all very deceptive: they come from the local clay and are about 50 million years old.

Rockery stones are often brought from distant quarries. A common choice is carboniferous limestone, a hard grey rock conspicuous in the Cheddar Gorge and Derbyshire, on which can often be seen white circular patterns with spokes, like feathery wheels; they stand out beautifully when the surface of the rock has been weathered a little. These are sections through fossil corals, and one is looking at a fossil coral reef formed about 250 million years ago in a clear warm sea. Portland stone is also popular for rockeries. Soon after moving into a house in Surrey I discovered that some of the Portland stones were crammed with fossils – particularly good specimens with which I enriched my collection at the expense of the rockery.

All this shows that it is not unusual to find fossils in the garden. Where there are rocks or gravel or clay there are usually fossils; finding them gives an added interest to gardening, and it is always worth while having them identified. You may even achieve fame in the newspapers: 'Mr Smith, while gardening at Crowstead, unearthed the skull of an extinct sea monster, said to be 150 million years old.' But it is far more likely to be a sea-urchin, very common and water-worn. Whether monster or sea-urchin, the wonder is there – and the sense of the continuity of life – that the roots of our garden plants should twine round the remains of inhabitants of the warm seas of æons ago.

A Trial of Strength   *by G. L. Carlisle*

THE crowd lining the bridge over the Thames was large even for a Saturday afternoon in July, and all were gazing intently at the water; so we stopped to have a look. Two swans were fighting.

'Wouldn't expect them to fight so late in the season, would you?' said one of the onlookers. 'Never seen the like of it in thirty years.'

'Been at it ten minutes or more,' I was told.

The cobs were in midstream just below the bridge. Their necks were crossed, and each was pecking at the other's wing in a rather desultory manner, doing no more than remove a few feathers. With wings outstretched on the water both birds maintained a continuous slow flapping. It was apparently a trial of strength in which each seemed to be struggling to get on top of his adversary.

After the fight had continued in one spot for several minutes the contestants began to drift downstream, a sign perhaps that one was tiring. A hundred yards beyond them a pen and seven cygnets emerged from the lee of an island and slowly advanced towards the scene of battle. At the same time one of the cobs succeeded in heaving his body across the other's wing, then suddenly got astride and shifted his beak grip to hold his opponent at the back of the head. Soon there was nothing of the other above water but his head. The wing splashing had ceased, all was quiet and the little white feathers sailed on. A murmur rose from the spectators, as if we all had the unpleasant feeling of witnessing a murder we were powerless to prevent.

Meanwhile the pen still approached apparently quite unperturbed, and the submerged cob somehow wriggled out from his position of near drowning to flap away upstream, pursued by the victor. Both scrambled ashore into reeds just below the bridge. There the engagement was broken off. One crashed through the undergrowth, regained the water beyond the bridge and made off up river. The other turned back, slid into the water and drifted away, preening himself and shaking his tail. He appeared too preoccupied to notice the pen and cygnets, which in turn were strangely unmoved by what had occurred.

A male red-throated diver gives his chick a lesson in eating.

The fish is dangled, seized and swallowed

Gannets nesting on Grassholm off the coast of Pembrokeshire

Harry the Seagull

by Pamela Hoare

I FIRST saw him when I was walking across the huge flat pebbles that litter the beach at Pennsylvania Cove in Dorset. He was perched on the knee of a middle-aged woman who sat placidly near the water's edge, surrounded by picnic baskets, towels, cameras and bathing suits. She appeared to be carrying on a conversation with him, as he gazed fixedly at her.

'Now then, Harry,' I heard as I came closer. 'What about a swim?' He put his head on one side and looked at her out of a shiny eye.

'George,' the woman called, and a boy who was kicking stones a little farther up the beach came towards her. 'Harry wants to go for a swim.'

'All right, Mum,' the boy cried. 'Tell him to wait a minute. I'll put on my trunks.'

Harry was a seagull, still with the brown and grey feathers of youth. I learnt how he had been brought by a fisherman who had found him on a ledge half-way down the cliffs. He was then about three weeks old; now he was nearly a year.

'And we can't get rid of him,' the woman went on, stroking Harry on the head. 'He sleeps in an old chicken house and goes everywhere with us.' She told me how he would disappear out of sight over the sea but always came back. 'Now you watch him go for a swim with George,' she said, shaking the bird off her knee as she spoke.

'Come along, Harry,' said George, and together they walked down to the water. Harry flew up a little, then dropped into the sea, rocking up and down on the waves. George drew in his toes at the water's edge, shivered and after some preliminary splashes and squeals went under. Boy and bird swam out together; but when George turned to come back

Harry rose from the water and flew in graceful widening curves farther and farther out.

George came dripping up the beach and rubbed himself dry, and I had begun to give up hope of seeing the bird again when I noticed a dark speck wheeling in across the bay. It was Harry. Down he planed, settling at last on the water a few feet from the shore. He landed a little farther down the beach and was no longer directly opposite the family.

'There now, look at him. He can't find us,' murmured Mum indulgently, as of a staggering infant son.

Harry ran in short dashes up and down the beach, looking this way and that, uttering faint agonized squawks and appearing like a frantic lost child. Then George stood up to pull on his trousers and the bird must have seen him, for he suddenly started to walk up the beach with that ungainly jerky step seagulls have when out of their native element.

Back in the family circle Harry perched on a cardboard box with string handles.

'That's what we carry him in,' said Mum. 'He goes everywhere with us. Proper lazy bird. Aren't you, ducks?' She smiled fondly at him, but he was already falling asleep. As his eyes closed and his head sunk into his feathers, George put him in his box.

DUCKING FOR BOTHA

Though our large Persian cat Botha was on the whole good-natured, he used to creep up behind the gulls on the beach below our house and spring at them, though without, to our knowledge, catching one or extracting even a single feather. This went on for a whole year, the cat becoming daily more wily. Once, however, as he lay asleep on the seawall a particularly large gull caught him unawares, picking him up by the scruff of the neck and carrying him out to sea. The bird swooped low over the water and ducked him several times before returning to the shore and dumping him in almost exactly the place where he had been lying. As I ran to his rescue the gull flew off.

The cat was under-weight at the time—more fur than anything else.

A. Collis Watson, Oxford

(Though it is tempting to suppose that the gull intended to teach the cat a lesson, it is as likely that it wanted a meal. – *R.F.*)

UNUSUAL CATCH

by G. E. B. de Maupas

One morning when I was aboard my boat putting grandfather prawns into the courge preparatory to a day with the bass, I was hailed by the harbourmaster on his way to his moorings. I sculled over to him and he showed me with pride a sunfish of about 18 lb., which he had caught that morning with a strip of mackerel, locally called a 'snaid', while fishing for pollack. In records extending over many years I have been able to find only four instances of a sunfish having been caught in this way, on a baited hook. The harbourmaster told me that he had cut open at least half a dozen taken in trammel nets and had found only seaweed in their stomachs.

As the illustration above shows, the sunfish looks rather like a fish cut in two and without its tail half. The back and fins are dark brown, and the belly a shining white. It has a very small mouth (probably one of the reasons why it is so rarely taken on a hook) and no teeth, though its gums are well coated with enamel. There is little sign of a tongue. Its beautiful eyes, rather like those of a deer, close if the pupil is touched. It may weigh up to 200 lb. but the flesh is too soft and watery for eating, or even for crab-pot bait. In summer these fish can often be seen off our south-west coast, floating or basking on the surface with their long dorsal fins and often their eyes out of the water. Sometimes they lie on one side, apparently asleep. In this position, they are regarded locally as a sign of fine calm weather. The name sunfish is apt too because of the white opalescent gleam of the almost circular body.

GULL OUTWITTED

I was watching a seagull gorging itself at a dish of food when three jackdaws appeared. They tried to snatch bits but had to make a hasty retreat as the gull pecked at them. After what looked like a conference two jackdaws paraded back and forth in front of the gull and, while its attention was taken, the third went behind and between the gull's legs to get a good feed in comparative safety. This worked several times, the jackdaws feeding in turns.

Joan Blewitt Cox, Devon

Sam Goes Fishing

by G. E. Wells

'IF that is all there is to catching a roach my dog could do it,' I said to the angler on the river bank, and the bet was on: a packet of dog biscuits to a pint of beer, the issue to be decided that afternoon.

When I arrived home I cut a 6-foot length of bamboo and, where the reel would normally come, I lashed a 6-inch length at right angles, so that Sam could hold the rod comfortably and firmly in his mouth. Possessing no line of my own, I had to borrow one, which I could not cut; I therefore fixed it to the tip of the rod, so that the baited hook would reach a foot or two below the surface of the water, and twisted the surplus round the bamboo as best I could. I made sure that there was no slack between the float and the end of the rod and reckoned that, by raising his head, Sam would be able to lift a fish out of the water and, with a slight toss of the head, land it. I made him practise the motions by sitting him on the bank and getting him to catch imaginary fish from the path. He could not see the point of all this but, keen to try anything, he did as he was asked with his usual enthusiasm.

After our midday meal I gathered up all the necessary paraphernalia and set off with Sam to the agreed meeting place by a lake that was seldom fished. The angler was there waiting for us, and I soon had Sam in position. Hardly was the line in the water before a fair-sized roach took the bait. Sam raised his head as previously instructed, but the fish was not properly hooked and, after leaping and wriggling in the air for a few seconds, it dropped back into the water, whereupon Sam threw down the rod and jumped in after the fish. He had a quick swim round, returned to the bank for scent and plunged in again. This time he put his head right underwater and pressed on till he was swimming below the surface. The angler doubled up with mirth, but Sam soon put a stop

Sam watches the float with intense interest, then he plunges after the fish that got away

He swings the fish he has caught to the bank. Like other fishermen, Sam poses with his catch

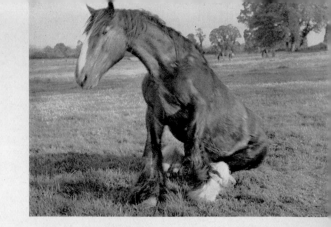

A tired horse lies down

to his laughter by clambering out and deluging him with spray.

Once more I explained to Sam the finer points of angling and started him off again with a freshly baited hook. The unexpected liveliness of the proceedings had caused the surplus line to come adrift; and to save Sam from becoming entangled in it I threw it into the rhododendron bushes behind him. Every now and again it became taut, merely adding to his difficulties, but he watched the float intently until it was again pulled under. This time he made his strike correctly. When the fish was clear of the water he shuffled and shivered with excitement and was on the point of springing to take it in his jaws; but he managed to control himself until the catch was still. Then he could not take his eye off it for the toss of the head that could complete the landing.

The angler insisted that, to win the bet, Sam must land the fish, and an impasse seemed to have been reached. At last Sam solved the problem by turning his head with a fleeting, comical glance of triumph in our direction, so swinging the fish sideways on to the bank. Then he posed with his catch and gear before we returned the fish to the lake.

HORSE FARE

When I stopped my car on the outskirts of a village to check the oil supply, a horse watched me from the paddock opposite. Suddenly he tore to the other end of the field and stood with his head over the fence, looking up the road. A small van soon appeared in the distance; as it approached, the horse flung his head back and kicked up his heels in excitement. The van slowed down as it drew level, and the horse trotted beside it back to my end of the field, where both came to a standstill. The driver then leaned out, popped an ice-cream cornet into the horse's mouth, revved up and was gone. The whole incident was timed to perfection. I learned afterwards that the ice-cream man blows a whistle at strategic points in the village. Evidently the horse listens and times the approach of the van accordingly. The daily titbit is a freewill offering. If the horse's owner has visitors, she takes them to see the performance and buys him an extra cornet, which he has now come to expect.

Stella Cosway, Berkshire

HARD-WORKING BEETLE

by C. T. L. Harrison

On a hillside in southern Italy, I was attracted by a subdued gnawing noise which was, I found, being made by a beetle about an inch long. It was cutting round the stump of a dead asphodel nearly 4 feet high, about 12 inches from the ground. When it had narrowed the stem to a small neck, it put its 'forehead' beneath the upper portion and tried to break this off. It pushed and strained, but could make the top move only slightly, so it resumed chewing and cut more away from the centre before pushing again. Eventually it managed to fell the stem, leaving the two pieces joined by a few fibres, which it quickly bit through. After that it pushed the top portion clear of the stump with its head. Then, without a pause, it began to bore a hole in the side of the remaining stump which faced due north. It worked at great speed and was soon boring away inside it. Late next day I found that the entrance hole had been sealed, so I slit the stem from the top down to the entrance hole with a sharp knife. Inside were five, or possibly six, identical chambers with an egg in each. These had been laid from the top downwards and a floor built in to make a separate chamber for each grub. The 'floors' had been made by the beetle, for it had first hollowed out the stem from bottom to top. I sealed up the stem with insulating tape and made one or two further examinations later to see how the grubs were developing. Unluckily, the day they hatched I was away. On my last visit I found that they had all emerged at the top, as the lowest floor and the seal of the entrance hole were intact. I was left wondering how the beetle measured the distance from the original cut to the entrance hole to get it exactly right. Did it pace it out or measure six lengths of its own body? The inside chambers, too, were identical in size.

Index

Page numbers in italics refer to illustrations

PHOTOGRAPHERS

Knots, Redshank, Oyster-catchers and Bar-tailed Godwit, Eric Hosking (*frontispiece*); *Pearl-bordered Fritillaries*, Gordon F. Woods 9; *Gadfly*, Ernst Zollinger 10; *Green Hairstreak*, Hermann Eisenbeiss 11; *Blues*, L. W. Newman 12; *White-letter Hairstreak*, G. E. Hyde 12; *Ichneumon-fly Grubs*, H. H. Goodchild 12; *Ladybird Swarm*, C. B. Williams 19; *Bee and Salvia* (3 photographs), Hermann Eisenbeiss 21–22; *Nightjar*, Robert Stenton 31; *Cock Reed-bunting*, S. McClelland 31; *Swifts* (4 photographs), H. N. Southern 32–33; *Sand-martins*, N. Duerden 34; *Swallows*, R. Wrigley 34; *Robin*, D. Jeffery 43; *Blue Tit*, Mark H. Waddicor 43; *Nest-boxes for Starlings*, A. Nove 43; *Tawny Owl*, W. Kenneth Richmond 44; *Perches for Migrant Birds*, John Bland 53; *Migrant Flycatchers*, G. J. Evans 53; *Long-eared Bat* (4 photographs), Sdeuard C. Bisserôt 54–55; *Mouse-eared Bat* (3 photographs), Jean McDougall 56; *Mole* (4 photographs), Colin G. Butler 65; *Hedgehog* (6 photographs), C. E. Owen 66; *Hamster* (5 photographs), Phyllis Moore 75; *Field Mice*, Ernst Zollinger 76–77; *Pine Martens* (4 photographs), H. G. Hurrell 78; *Racoons*, Francis Dickie 87; *Badger*, Ernest G. Neal 87; *Fox Cub*, George Nicolle 88; *Sika Deer, Indian Muntjac Deer*, Zoological Society 97; *Roe Deer and Yearling Buck*, Peter Delap 98–99; *Red Deer*, T. Weir 100; *Common Toads*, George Pallister 109; *Eel*, Ernst Zollinger 110; *Jersey Crocus*, Douglas P. Wilson 115; *Pasque Flower*, J. C. Faulkner 115; *Stinkhorn Fungus* (4 photographs), D. Swinscow 116; *Swans* (3 photographs), G. L. Carlisle 121; *Red-throated Diver and Chick* (4 photographs), Alex Tewnion 122–123; *Gannets*, Alasdair Alpin Macgregor 124; *Sunfish*, G. E. B. de Maupas 127; *Black Retriever* (4 photographs), G. E. Wells 129; *Horse* (3 photographs), Watkins 130.

ARTISTS

The drawings on pages 26, 37, 38 and 48 are by R. A. Richardson; on page 16 by C. B. Williams; on pages 39, 40 and 41 by E. M. Barraud; on pages 60, 61, 62 and 64 by Lawrence Leeks; on page 103 by Maurice Wilson; on page 114 by L. Foest; on pages 118 and 119 by Duncan Forbes; and on page 132 by M. Rivers Moore.